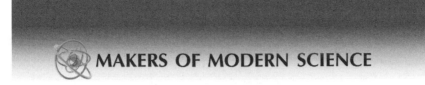

MAKERS OF MODERN SCIENCE

Robert
Ballard

MAKERS OF MODERN SCIENCE

Robert Ballard

Explorer and Undersea Archaeologist

LISA YOUNT

CHELSEA HOUSE
PUBLISHERS
An imprint of Infobase Publishing

ROBERT BALLARD: Explorer and Undersea Archaeologist

Copyright © 2009 by Lisa Yount

Chelsea House
An imprint of Infobase Publishing
132 West 31st Street
New York NY 10001

Library of Congress Cataloging-in-Publication Data

Yount, Lisa.
   Robert Ballard : explorer and undersea archaeologist / Lisa Yount.
      p. cm.—(Makers of modern science)
   Includes bibliographical references and index.
   ISBN-13: 978-0-8160-6173-0
   ISBN-10: 0-8160-6173-4
   1. Ballard, Robert D. 2. Oceanographers—United States—Biography—Juvenile literature. 3. Explorers—United States—Biography—Juvenile literature. I. Title. II. Series.
   GC30.B35Y56 2009
   551.46092—dc22
[B]   2008039983

Text design by Kerry Casey
Cover design by Salvatore Luongo
Illustrations by Sholto Ainslie
Photo research by Suzanne M. Tibor

Printed in the United States of America

MP KT 10 9 8 7 6 5 4 3 2 1

This book is printed on acid-free paper.

To all young people
who want to explore the world

CONTENTS

PREFACE

S cience is, above all, a great human adventure. It is the process of exploring what Albert Einstein called the "magnificent structure" of nature using observation, experience, and logic. Science comprises the best methods known to humankind for finding reliable answers about the unknown. With these tools, scientists probe the great mysteries of the universe—from black holes and star nurseries to deep-sea hydrothermal vents (and extremophile organisms that survive high temperatures to live in them); from faraway galaxies to subatomic particles such as quarks and antiquarks; from signs of life on other worlds to microorganisms such as bacteria and viruses here on Earth; from how a vaccine works to protect a child from disease to the DNA, genes, and enzymes that control traits and processes from the color of a boy's hair to how he metabolizes sugar.

Some people think that science is rigid and static, a dusty, musty set of facts and statistics to memorize for a test and then forget. Some think of science as antihuman—devoid of poetry, art, and a sense of mystery. However, science is based on a sense of wonder and is all about exploring the mysteries of life and our planet and the vastness of the universe. Science offers methods for testing and reasoning that help keep us honest with ourselves. As physicist Richard Feynman once said, science is above all a way to keep from fooling yourself—or letting nature (or others) fool you. Nothing could be more growth-oriented or more human. Science evolves continually. New bits of knowledge and fresh discoveries endlessly shed light and open perspectives. As a result, science is constantly undergoing revolutions—ever refocusing what scientists have explored before into fresh, new understanding. Scientists like to say science is self-correcting. That is, science is fallible, and scientists can be wrong. It is easy to fool yourself, and it is easy to be fooled by others, but because new facts are constantly flowing in, scientists are continually refining their work to account for as many facts as possible. So science can make mistakes, but it also can correct itself.

Sometimes, as medical scientist Jonas Salk liked to point out, good science thrives when scientists ask the right question about what they observe. "What people think of as the moment of discovery is really the discovery of the question," he once remarked.

There is no one, step-by-step "scientific method" that all scientists use. However, science requires the use of methods that are systematic, logical, and *empirical* (based on objective observation and experience). The goal of science is to explore and understand how nature works—what causes the patterns, the shapes, the colors, the textures, the consistency, the mass, and all the other characteristics of the natural universe that we see.

What is it like to be a scientist? Many people think of stereotypes of the scientist trapped in cold logic or the cartoonlike "mad" scientists. In general, these portrayals are more imagination than truth. Scientists use their brains. They are exceptionally good at logic and critical thinking. This is where the generalizations stop. Although science follows strict rules, it is often guided by the many styles and personalities of the scientists themselves, who have distinct individuality, personality, and style. What better way to explore what science is all about than through the experiences of great scientists?

Each volume of the Makers of Modern Science series presents the life and work of a prominent scientist whose outstanding contributions have garnered the respect and recognition of the world. These men and women were all great scientists, but they differed in many ways. Their approaches to the use of science were different: Niels Bohr was an atomic theorist whose strengths lay in patterns, ideas, and conceptualization, while Wernher von Braun was a hands-on scientist/engineer who led the team that built the giant rocket used by Apollo astronauts to reach the Moon. Some's genius was sparked by solitary contemplation—geneticist Barbara McClintock worked alone in fields of maize and sometimes spoke to no one all day long. Others worked as members of large, coordinated teams. Oceanographer Robert Ballard organized oceangoing ship crews on submersible expeditions to the ocean floor; biologist Jonas Salk established the Salk Institute to help scientists in different fields collaborate more freely and study the human body through the interrelationships of their differing knowledge and approaches. Their personal styles also differed: biologist Rita Levi-Montalcini enjoyed wearing chic dresses and makeup; McClintock was sunburned and wore baggy denim jeans and an oversized shirt; nuclear physicist Richard Feynman was a practical joker and an energetic bongo drummer.

The scientists chosen represent a spectrum of disciplines and a diversity of approaches to science as well as lifestyles. Each biography explores the scientist's younger years along with education and growth as a scientist; the experiences, research, and contributions of the maturing scientist; and the course of the path to recognition. Each volume also explores the nature of science and its unique usefulness for studying the universe and contains sidebars covering related facts or profiles of interest, introductory coverage of the scientist's field, line illustrations and photographs, a time line, a glossary of related scientific terms, and a list of further resources including books, Web sites, periodicals, and associations.

The volumes in the Makers of Modern Science series offer a factual look at the lives and exciting contributions of the profiled scientists in the hope that readers will see science as a uniquely human quest to understand the universe and that some readers may be inspired to follow in the footsteps of these great scientists.

ACKNOWLEDGMENTS

I would like to thank Frank K. Darmstadt for his help and suggestions, Suzie Tibor for her hard work in rounding up the photographs, my cats for keeping me company (helpfully or otherwise), and, as always, my husband, Harry Henderson, for—well—everything.

INTRODUCTION

"In an era when climbing Mt. Everest is just a matter of laying out the right amount of cash," Eli Lehrer wrote in an article about Robert Ballard that appeared in the May 3, 1999, *Insight on the News,* "authentic explorers are few and far between. Robert Ballard is one of them."

Ballard would certainly seem to have earned the right to this compliment. Arguably the most well-traveled undersea explorer of all time, he has taken part in more than a hundred expeditions. He codiscovered the most famous of modern shipwrecks, RMS *Titanic,* and created detailed photographic records of this and dozens of other deepwater wrecks. He took part in several of the most important discoveries made in marine science during the second half of the 20th century and essentially founded a new scientific subfield, deepsea archaeology.

What Is an Explorer?

But what is an authentic explorer—and why should Robert Ballard be given that title?

Many people picture explorers, especially explorers like Ballard, who specialize in archaeology, as being similar to movie hero Indiana Jones. Such people supposedly dash into hidden caves or strongholds, battle evildoers, seize the precious artifacts for which they came, then dash out again without a backward glance.

Robert Ballard's life is not like that. He has engaged in battles of sorts, and at times he has risked his life to reach his goals. His battles, however, were not with villainous Nazis or Soviet agents but with balky underwater machinery or, occasionally, pushy reporters or obstructive bureaucrats. The threats to his life have come not from pistols,

Robert Ballard has been called one of the modern world's few authentic explorers. He took part in several major discoveries in marine science, invented robot devices for exploring the deep sea, and photographed the remains of RMS Titanic and a host of other important shipwrecks. (Kip Evans Photography)

explosives, or even (as in Jones's case) snakes, but from the cold, dark, unrelenting deep sea—perhaps the most hostile environment on Earth—where pressure can be measured in tons per square inch.

Above all, Ballard, unlike Jones, does not snatch his treasures and run. In most of his expeditions, he has retrieved no artifacts from his sites at all. When he has removed objects, he has done so at the request of professional archaeologists who need them for research. (Lacking an academic degree in archaeology, Ballard is careful to call himself "an underwater explorer" rather than an archaeologist or a historian.) Before touching the artifacts, he carefully documented their exact location on the sites. Ballard has repeatedly spoken out against salvagers who remove artifacts carelessly, especially those who take them for profit.

Explorers "sail off the map" of the known world, steering toward uncharted destinations. Robert Ballard has certainly done that. "Ballard, whose best ideas tend to be about 22 years ahead of their time, is accustomed to sailing upwind [against prevailing forces]," Peter de Jonge wrote in a profile of Ballard that appeared in the May 2004 *National Geographic.* Explorers also often set multiple goals so that they can turn to a new plan quickly after an old one fails or is completed. Ballard, whom de Jonge calls "a compulsively restless visionary," does this as well. "By the time he realizes one vision, he is already hatching the next one or the one after that."

Explorers must be willing to break away from predicted paths, even when the paths from which they diverge are those that they have set up for themselves. Robert Ballard has changed the course of his life several times in order to go where his interests and instincts led him. He earned a Ph.D. in marine geology, but in midlife he left this field and focused instead on archaeology and history. He became an expert on submersibles (miniature submarines), logging more time in the tiny craft than any other scientist, yet he eventually decided that robotic remotely operated vehicles (ROVs) were better tools for undersea exploration. He investigated 20th-century shipwrecks for years and then decided to concentrate on wrecks that were far older. He turned from conventional scientific writing, aimed mostly at other scientists, to books, articles, and lectures created for the general public and even for children.

Inventor and Persuader

Because explorers often find themselves in unique environments, they must be resourceful enough to invent the tools they need to survive in those environments and achieve their goals. This, too, Robert Ballard has done. Before his time, undersea archaeologists could explore sunken ships or other underwater sites only if the sites lay less than 200 feet (61 m) below the surface, the maximum depth to which a scuba diver could go. (Manned submersibles could travel deeper, but their ability to view and photograph sites was limited.) Ballard invented a series of undersea robots that can send video feeds to their operators in real time or take thousands of color photographs of a wreck, creating a mosaic that shows every detail in its proper location.

These tools have made underwater exploration of all kinds safer. Instead of being crammed into the tiny personnel sphere of a submersible, surrounded by an environment that would instantly destroy them if it should penetrate their fortress, the operators of ROVs manipulate the devices from the relative comfort of a control van on a surface ship—yet they see as much as if they personally were on the ocean floor. Marine scientists and the military as well as undersea archaeologists have welcomed Ballard's advances in what he calls "telepresence."

Explorers can seldom achieve their goals completely on their own, so they must persuade others to share their dreams. They have to gather both skilled crews to help them carry out their expeditions and backers to provide the financial support that makes the expeditions possible. When they return, they must convince their supporters—and perhaps a larger public audience as well—that their journeys and discoveries were worthwhile.

Robert Ballard has always possessed this power of persuasion. As a young man, he gathered support for the new technology of submersibles so vigorously that colleagues compared him to a tornado. He convinced sources as diverse as the U.S. Navy, the National Geographic Society, and television networks to fund his explorations. He assembled experts from numerous institutions to accompany him as well as created his own veteran teams. He called opinion leaders and legislators to support his drive for preservation of undersea wrecks and taught students around the world to share his fascination with history and science. Indeed, he has shared his enthusiasm and achievements with the public so effectively that he has been labeled the world's most famous living oceanographer.

To be sure, Ballard's pursuit of public attention has sometimes displeased fellow scientists. In a January 1987 *Discover* article about Ballard, Barry Raleigh, then director of Columbia University's Lamont-Doherty Geological Observatory, stated that Ballard's discovery of *Titanic* and its attendant publicity was "not science" but merely "hoopla." Ballard insists, however, that he has always made the entertainment aspect of his presentations serve the ends of science and history, and others apparently have agreed. The National Geographic Society gave him its highest award, the Hubbard Medal, in 1996 for "extraordinary accomplishments in coaxing secrets from the world's oceans and engaging students in the wonder of science." Other prizes given to Ballard include the Underwater Society of America's Science Award (1976), the Westinghouse Award from the American Association for the Advancement of Science (1990), and the National Humanities Medal from the National Endowment for the Humanities (2003).

Robert Ballard himself has defined exploration, and in doing so, he has defined himself as explorer. He wrote the following in *Return to Midway*:

> To explore means to search for something bigger than yourself. It means measuring yourself against challenges that are both physical and mental. The need to explore the frontier, whatever that may be at a given moment in history, is fundamental to the human experience.

Most of Ballard's expeditions have succeeded in their aims, but like all true explorers, he sees exploration as meaning far more than success. "I would rather fail while exploring than fail by never having tried," he wrote in another book, *Graveyards of the Pacific*. "I'm in this for the journey—as much as for the destination.

"After all, that's what exploration is."

Map of a Career

Existing maps cannot show an explorer's travels. Instead, journeys of exploration give birth to new maps that guide the generations who follow. This volume in the Makers of Modern Science series maps the best known of Robert Ballard's travels in the hope that doing so will help young people share the excitement about exploration and science that Ballard himself has expressed so well in his books, television programs, and educational projects.

Chapters 1 and 2 describe Ballard's youth and early career as a marine geologist. Chapter 1 traces his development from boyhood in southern California to professional life on North America's opposite coast, a change of location brought about by the U.S. Navy. This chapter also pictures Ballard's first underwater experiences and his growing expertise in the new technology of submersibles. As chapter 2 reveals, Ballard took part in several key discoveries in marine science during the 1970s, including direct proof of the theory of plate tectonics and the first sightings of hot-water vents, surrounded by colonies of unique organisms, on the deep sea floor.

Ballard's most famous expedition, which found the remains of the luxury liner RMS *Titanic* in 1985, is described in chapter 3, as is his return for a more detailed examination of the wreck in 1986. These expeditions marked major changes in Ballard's career, from marine geology to deepwater archaeology, and in his technological interests, from submersibles to remotely operated vehicles. His discovery of *Titanic* and the fame it brought him also inspired a new interest in education, as the first part of chapter 4 recounts.

The remainder of the book outlines Ballard's most famous undersea archaeology expeditions in the years following his investigation of *Titanic*. Many of these expeditions have centered on shipwrecks that played important parts in World Wars I and II. The chapters tell the stories of the ships themselves and the battles that ended their lives as well as describing Ballard's journeys to photograph them on the seafloor.

In addition to portraying the birth of Ballard's educational program, the JASON Project, chapter 4 presents his discovery of the

German battleship *Bismarck,* which British warships sank in the North Atlantic in May 1941. Chapters 5 and 6 recount Ballard's visits to shipwrecks on the sites of several important World War II battles in the Pacific Ocean, including Guadalcanal, Midway, and Pearl Harbor, as well as another ocean liner, *Lusitania,* that was sunk in the Atlantic during the early days of World War I. Ballard's recent shift in focus from modern to ancient shipwrecks is described in chapter 7.

The book's conclusion presents one of Robert Ballard's most recent expeditions, a return visit to *Titanic* that he made in 2004. It reproduces his impassioned call for laws to protect historically important shipwrecks, which was spurred by the considerable damage caused by salvagers that his photographs revealed. Finally, it describes Ballard's greatest hope—that the great museum of the deep sea someday will be opened to the world, allowing not only explorers like himself but everyone to experience the history that lies within.

1

Growing Up Nemo

Like Dorothy Gale, the heroine of L. Frank Baum's fantasies about the mystical land of Oz, Robert Duane Ballard was born in Kansas—specifically in Wichita, on June 30, 1942. His family had history in the town: His father's father, a U.S. marshal, was killed in a gunfight there, and Ballard himself once said, "You could call me a high-tech cowboy."

A Seaside Boyhood

"Cowboy" though he might have been by birth, Ballard grew up in an environment very different from the Midwest—the southern California seaside city of San Diego. Chester Ballard, his father, an aerospace executive and missile engineer; the former Harriet May, his mother; and their three children moved there when Bob was just a baby. In his boyhood a different fantasy inspired him, one

Jules Verne's 19th-century science-fiction novel 20,000 Leagues Under the Sea, *featuring the adventures of Captain Nemo (shown here) in his submarine* Nautilus, *made Robert Ballard dream of exploring the deep sea.* (Archival photography by Steve Nicklas, NOS, NGS/National Oceanic and Atmospheric Administration/Department of Commerce)

that fitted his new home—Jules Verne's *20,000 Leagues under the Sea,* first published in 1870. Bob Ballard grew up wanting to explore the deep sea like Nemo, the mysterious captain of the submarine *Nautilus* in Verne's story.

Real adventures on the sea inspired Ballard as well. He heard about plenty of them from his father and his father's friends in the navy. In those years during and just after World War II (1941–45), San Diego was filled with navy personnel, and stories about naval battles were on everyone's lips. Ballard also read accounts of lost ships such as *Titanic,* a British luxury liner that hit an iceberg in the North Atlantic and sank on the night of April 14, 1912, costing 1,522 lives.

Bob himself spent as much time in and around the ocean as he could. He played at the end of a pier located just a block from his home, admiring the mussels, barnacles, crabs, and other sea creatures that clung to its submerged pilings or swam in the nearby tidepools. He surfed, fished, snorkeled, and eventually dove with scuba gear. "I decided . . . that I never wanted to be far from the water," Ballard told *Discover* magazine writer Frederic Golden in 1987.

As Ballard grew older, he learned about scientists who studied the sea, working from such bases as the Scripps Institution of Oceanography in nearby La Jolla. In 1959, when he was a senior in high school, Ballard wrote to Scripps asking what he could do to learn more about the ocean. The scientist who answered his letter sent him an application for a summer program that the institution sponsored, and Ballard signed up. The program included two short trips on Scripps research vessels, which introduced him (as he wrote in *Explorations,* his autobiography) to "the ceaseless drudgery of round-the-clock data collection and the discomfort of bad weather on a crowded ship." Even so, Ballard's summer's experience convinced him that he wanted to become a marine scientist.

Changing Plans

On the advice of one of his Scripps mentors, Ballard went to college at the University of California campus in Santa Barbara, another seaside city further up the coast. He chose the unusual double major of chemistry and geology and graduated with a degree in physical sciences in 1965.

Ballard continued his seaside schooling at the University of Hawaii in Honolulu. He had decided by this time that undersea geology was the ocean science that interested him most, so he studied in the university's institute of geophysics. To earn money for his tuition, he took a part-time job as a dolphin trainer for an amusement park called Sea Life Park. "Actually," Ballard commented in *Explorations,* "it would have been fairer to describe my work with spotted dolphins and rough-toothed porpoises as those clever animals training *me."*

Ballard changed his study plans in summer 1966 when he obtained a position with North American Aviation's Ocean Systems Group. He already knew the company well, since his father was one of its vice presidents, and he himself had worked there in a summer job several years before. The Ocean Systems Group's headquarters were in Long Beach, so he knew he would need to return to California. He had been dating an "adventuresome" young woman named Marjorie Hargas while in Hawaii, and they could not bear to part, so she came with him. They were married soon afterward.

Ballard's job with North American, he wrote later, was "one of the best jobs any aspiring ocean scientist could imagine." He was part of a team assigned to develop ideas for using the *Beaver Mark IV,* a manned submersible (small submarine) that the company was in the process of building. Submersibles, a new and promising tool for undersea exploration, allowed researchers to reach relatively great depths and to maneuver easily once they arrived. At the same time that he worked for the company, Ballard continued his graduate work in geology and geophysics at the University of Southern California (USC), where North American paid for his tuition.

The U.S. military, however, had other plans for Ballard. While in college, he had joined the army's Reserve Officers Training Corps (ROTC) program, and when he graduated, he was made a second lieutenant in the army intelligence service. He knew that his commitment for active duty would be postponed until he finished graduate school, but while he was in Hawaii, he became nervous about what that commitment might involve. The United States was heavily engaged in the Vietnam War (1959–75) at the time. Ballard wrote in *Explorations* that he was not afraid to go to Vietnam and did not oppose the war, but stories he heard from friends who were already serving in the intelligence service overseas convinced him that "duty as a combat intel[ligence] officer in this particular war involved treating Viet Cong [enemy] suspects in ways I never intended to treat any human being." Transferring to the navy, he thought, might help him avoid this dilemma. Joining the navy also made sense because of his fascination with the sea. Arranging the transfer took some discussion, but he eventually succeeded.

Ballard had assumed that the navy, like the army, would let him postpone active duty as long as he stayed in graduate school. Unfortunately for his plans, navy officials had not learned that he was enrolled at USC or that he had married. They knew only that he had left the University of Hawaii—which meant that, as far as they were concerned, he was available for active duty immediately. One night early in 1967, a navy lieutenant appeared at his Long Beach apartment and told him that he had to report for duty in 30 days.

The "White Tornado"

Ballard learned that he had been assigned to the Office of Naval Research (ONR) as the scientific liaison officer between ONR and Woods Hole Oceanographic Institution (WHOI), an institution much like Scripps that was located on the southwestern corner of Cape Cod in Massachusetts. Ballard and Marjorie therefore packed up their most important possessions and drove across the country to Boston.

Ballard began to work at Woods Hole in March. Most of his job was simply bureaucratic paperwork. It was important, however, because all requests that WHOI scientists made for ONR funding had to pass through him. Such requests were frequent. Unlike Scripps, affiliated with the University of California at San Diego, and the country's third well-known oceanographic research institution, Columbia University's Lamont Geological Observatory (later the Lamont-Doherty Earth Observatory), WHOI was not attached to a university. The institution therefore had to find other sources of income, and, at that time, ONR and other navy agencies provided 85 percent of its financial support.

The navy in those days was often generous with its research grants. The important role of submarines in World War II and the ongoing "cold war," an intense rivalry between the United States and the Soviet Union that threatened to erupt into military combat at any time, had made U.S. military leaders extremely interested in oceanography. Furthermore, the race into outer space filled the day's newspaper headlines, and many marine scientists hoped that the country's fascination with exploration of so-called final frontiers would spill over into their field, creating a "wet NASA"—an

Alvin: **Workhorse Submersible**

Officially, the submersible *Alvin* was named after Allyn Vine (1914–94), the WHOI geophysicist and engineer whose enthusiasm for submersibles was chiefly responsible for its creation. Legend at Woods Hole, however, holds that the name was also inspired by a chipmunk who was the hero of a popular song and, later, a television cartoon.

The sub itself was no laughing matter. Launched in 1964, three years before Robert Ballard came to WHOI, it was 22 feet (6.6 m) long and eight feet (2.4 m) wide. Made of Fiberglas, a strong, lightweight material composed of spun-glass fibers, its white hull had a protruding top part called a conning tower or sail; a large propeller on the rear and two smaller ones on the sides; and a stainless-steel manipulator arm, ending in a pincer or claw, on one side. Its passenger sphere, which held three people, was made from an exceptionally strong alloy of steel so that it could withstand the tremendous pressure of the deep sea. The steel sphere was replaced with one of titanium, an even stronger material, in 1973.

The most spectacular early demonstration of *Alvin*'s powers came in 1966 after a U.S. Air Force B-52 bomber carrying four hydrogen bombs on a standard cold-war patrol collided with a tanker plane over the coast of Spain. One of the four bombs, not primed to explode but carrying a nuclear warhead, fell into the sea, causing panic both inside and outside the military. *Alvin* played a key part in the search that eventually led to the safe recovery of the bomb.

Alvin served the marine science community for 40 years, performing more than 4,000 dives. Robert Ballard used the submersible during several of his most important expeditions, including the ocean-science program as wide ranging and well funded as those run by the National Aeronautics and Space Administration.

Ballard, now an ensign in a white navy uniform, took on his job at WHOI with such energy that he soon earned the nickname of "White Tornado," after a popular cleaning product that commercials compared to a whirlwind. In addition to handling ONR business, he continued his graduate training informally by joining WHOI scientists on research cruises and writing his first scientific papers under their watchful eyes.

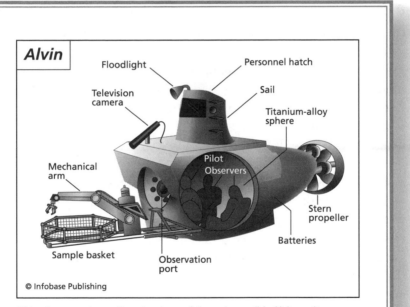

Alvin

Floodlight

Personnel hatch

Television camera

Sail

Titanium-alloy sphere

Mechanical arm

Pilot Observers

Stern propeller

Batteries

Sample basket

Observation port

© Infobase Publishing

This diagram shows the structure of the submersible Alvin *as it was in 1975. A second manipulator arm and other features, including a stronger hull, were added later.*

ones that examined the Mid-Atlantic Ridge, discovered the bizarre animals and "smoking" mineral chimneys that surround hot-water vents on the deep sea floor, and photographed the wreckage of *Titanic*. The odd-looking little vessel carried hundreds of other scientists into the deep sea as well, taking part in many of the major discoveries in late 20th-century oceanography.

Hard Times

WHOI had several surface ships devoted to research, but the center-piece of its oceanographic activities was its new small submersible, *Alvin*, just a few years old at the time that Ballard took up his post. ONR had paid for *Alvin*'s development and in fact owned the craft, but WHOI operated it under lease from the navy. In *Explorations*, Ballard described the little sub as "a bulbous Fiberglas pollywog." Still, he admitted that he felt an attachment to the little vessel the minute he saw it on his first day at Woods Hole.

Ballard hoped for a chance to dive in the odd little craft, but for a while it seemed as if that might never happen. On October 16, 1968, the support cables that attached *Alvin* to its mother ship, *Lulu*, broke just as the submersible was being launched for a dive. *Alvin* slipped into the sea with its hatch still open, filled with water, and sank out of sight as the three men who had been in the process of boarding it scrambled to safety. It remained on the sea bottom, 5,000 feet (1,515 m) down, until September 1969, when it was finally raised and brought back to WHOI.

Before it could be recovered, the hapless submersible suffered a second catastrophe, this time financial. Hopes for a "wet NASA" were fading as the ongoing Vietnam War sucked up more and more of the military's budget, leaving little for scientific exploration. The ONR told WHOI in August 1969 that its funding for *Alvin* would probably end in a few years. The institute was by no means sure that the submersible could continue to operate without that support, even if they could retrieve and repair it.

The budget cuts that threatened to end *Alvin*'s career did the same for Robert Ballard. A month after navy officials brought their bad news about the submersible to WHOI, they told Ballard that he would either have to sign up as a career officer in the regular navy or find other employment. Ballard knew he wanted a career in ocean science and not in the military, but by this time he had a child as well as a wife to consider: His first son, Todd, had been born the previous July. He also needed a way to pay for the rest of the schooling he would need to obtain his Ph.D.

William Rainnie, the head of the WHOI group that managed *Alvin*, thought that Ballard and the submersible might be able to solve one another's problems. It was clear that WHOI would have to start charging scientists and institutions for using *Alvin*, but this would not be an easy task; many marine researchers doubted the value and safety of submersibles and had not been persuaded to board the craft even when it was offered for free. Rainnie believed that Ballard, the "White Tornado," had exactly the sort of energy and enthusiasm that a salesman for time on the submersible would need. He therefore offered Ballard a job as a WHOI fund-raiser.

Ballard thought this was a perfect idea, since he had become firmly convinced by this time that the future of ocean research lay with submersibles like *Alvin*. By allowing scientists to travel personally into the deep sea to observe and collect specimens, he thought, submersibles could provide a "hands-on" approach that would never be possible with devices lowered from surface ships. He joined WHOI as a research associate in engineering in 1970 when his navy commission ended.

Unfortunately, the same job that cured the economic half of Ballard's woes made the academic half worse. He had planned to work for his doctorate at WHOI, but he was now told that he could not do so because he was a Woods Hole employee. Luckily, however, another friend whom Ballard had made at WHOI, marine geologist K. O. Emery, arranged for him to enroll in a Ph.D. program in marine geology at the nearby University of Rhode Island. Ballard had completed most of his required graduate classes earlier in Hawaii and California, so he would have to spend very little time at the university. It was agreed that he would do his thesis research at WHOI.

First Dive

In December 1969, just a few months after these major readjustments in his career, Ballard finally had his first chance to travel under the sea. He did not go in *Alvin*, which was still undergoing repairs after its unexpected dunking, but in a larger submersible, the *Ben Franklin*. This craft had been designed by undersea explorer Jacques Piccard (1922–), who in 1960, with navy submarine officer Donald Walsh (1931–), had set the record for the world's deepest dive—35,800 feet (10,668 m) down in the Mariana Trench, near the

Plate Tectonics: A Revolutionary Theory

The plate-tectonics theory was the Cinderella of earth science. It began in 1915 when Alfred Wegener (1880–1930), a German meteorologist (weather scientist), published a book called *The Origin of Continents and Oceans.* In that book, Wegener proposed that Earth's landmasses had changed their positions on the planet's surface over geologic time. They began as a single mass, Pangaea ("all-Earth"), about 250 million years ago and then slowly split apart, impelled by forces that Wegener could hardly define.

Wegener was respected as a meteorologist and Arctic explorer (he died on his fourth expedition to Greenland), but most geologists ridiculed his theory, which came to be called continental drift. They believed that landmasses might have risen or sunk relative to the oceans, but they could not imagine any reasons why the continents would have moved sideways.

A few geologists began to reconsider Wegener's ideas in the early 1960s. Researchers had discovered that a chain of gigantic undersea mountains, the Mid-Ocean Ridge, snaked through the center of the world's oceans like the curving seam on a baseball. This ridge, split down the middle by a rift valley, was the site of frequent earthquakes. Building on the ideas of one of Wegener's few earlier supporters, British geologist Arthur Holmes (1890–1965), a U.S. geologist, Harry Hess (1906–69) proposed in 1960 that currents in the mantle, the molten layer beneath Earth's crust, pulled the seafloor apart in the mid-ocean rift valleys. Liquid lava bubbled up through the cracks and hardened when it contacted the cold seawater, forming new land that was slowly pushed to both sides of the ridge. At other weak spots in the crust, usually near chains of islands and deep gashes in the seafloor called trenches, gravity pulled pieces of crust back into the mantle. These "conveyor belt" movements of the crust carried the continental landmasses along with them, producing changes something like those Wegener had described.

At first, Hess's theory was no more accepted than Wegener's had been. Within a few years, however, earth scientists using several kinds of new or improved technology began to find evidence that supported it. For example, researchers measuring magnetic fields on the sea floor found alternating "stripes" of normal and reversed magnetism that ran parallel to several sections of the Mid-Ocean Ridge. If, as other scientists were then proposing, Earth's magnetic field had reversed its direction periodically during the geologic past,

German meteorologist
(weather scientist) Alfred
Wegener, shown here,
was known chiefly as an
Arctic explorer during his
lifetime. Most contempo-
raries rejected his theory
of continental drift, which
held that landmasses had
moved horizontally on the
Earth's surface during
geologic time. However,
Wegener's theory inspired
a later one, called plate
tectonics, which is
now widely accepted.
(Archive/Alfred-Wegener-
Institut, Germany)

this pattern was exactly what Hess's seafloor spreading would be
expected to produce.

A Canadian geophysicist, John Tuzo Wilson (1908–93), in turn
built on Hess's theory. In 1965, Wilson proposed that Earth's crust
was divided into a number of rigid plates. The creation and destruction of crust beneath the sea, as described by Hess, made these
plates move relative to one another. Earthquakes and volcanic
activity racked the plates' borders as they collided or scraped past
one another.

By 1967, evidence supporting the ideas of Hess and Wilson
(and, indirectly, Wegener) had become so powerful that many
earth scientists decided that the theories had to be accepted. The
ideas were pulled together into a single theory that came to be
called plate tectonics (from a Greek word meaning "to build"). Most
historians of science say that the sudden shift from rejection to
acceptance of plate tectonics was a true scientific revolution. It was
probably the most important change in earth science during the
20th century.

South Pacific island of Guam. They traveled in a huge vessel called a bathyscaphe, which consisted of a small steel passenger sphere suspended from a large float that contained gasoline for buoyancy.

The *Ben Franklin* was quite different from Piccard's bathyscaphe, the *Trieste*. It was far more maneuverable, but it could not go nearly as deep. Piccard called it a mesoscaphe, or "middle boat." It was the submersible equivalent of a luxury liner, with eight comfortable bunks for crew members and even an observation lounge. Piccard had already used it on an extensive cruise in 1968 to measure the powerful ocean current called the Gulf Stream. The cruise ran along the east coast of North America from West Palm Beach, Florida, to southern Nova Scotia, Canada.

The research trip that Ballard joined was briefer, a short dive to conduct a geological and biological survey of the continental shelf near the submersible's home port at West Palm Beach. The craft went down a mere 541 feet (165 m), but the journey thrilled him because he saw it as the first fulfillment of his "Captain Nemo" dream. The shallow tropical water at the *Ben Franklin*'s first dive station, 115 feet (35 m) below the surface, swarmed with colorful fish and reminded him of illustrations in the Verne book. The deeper ocean floor, however, was grim and barren: a sediment-covered plain occupied only by occasional sea cucumbers (a simple type of sea animal without a backbone) and dead-white crabs that scavenged the bottom for organic debris that floated down from above.

Mapping Undersea Mountains

For his Ph.D. project, Ballard decided to investigate a new theory called plate tectonics, which had recently caused a revolution in the earth sciences. Although many scientists had come to accept this theory, it was still controversial; in *Explorations*, Ballard wrote that arguments about it amounted to "the scientific equivalent of a civil war." More evidence therefore was needed to establish its truth.

According to plate tectonics, North America and Europe had once been part of the same landmass. Therefore, certain chains of mountains and other rock formations in northeastern North America were expected to continue underwater to the edge of the continental shelf and then to resume on the continental shelf and coast of northwestern Europe. This appeared to be true for the Appalachian Mountains in the United States and Canada, which continued as the Caledonian Range in Scotland and northwestern Europe. Information about parts of the chain that lay below sea level had been lacking, however.

Ballard focused on a rock formation in the Appalachians termed the Newark Group. This formation lay partly underwater in the Gulf of Maine north of Cape Cod, where the Appalachians continued as an undersea range that ran down the slope of the continental shelf. Ballard hoped to map the underwater part of the formation and obtain rock samples from it. He could then compare information from the maps and samples with what was known about land rocks in the Appalachians and the Caledonian chain. If the features of the undersea rocks matched those of the land rocks, his work would add to the evidence supporting plate tectonics.

Alvin was still being repaired, but Ballard did not want to start his research in the submersible in any case. He had come to believe that because submersibles such as *Alvin* could not sweep wide areas easily, they were most useful when they could be sent to precise, pre-determined locations rather than being used as exploration vehicles. On the other hand, *Lulu*, *Alvin*'s mother ship, was available, and Ballard knew he could use devices aboard that craft to map the rock formations on the floor of the gulf. With these maps in hand, he would know exactly where to take *Alvin* if he later had the chance to use the sub for collecting rock samples.

Ballard made several cruises on *Lulu* in 1970. *Lulu* was a strange-looking vessel, consisting primarily of two salvaged World War II minesweeping pontoons (long, flat-bottomed vessels) welded together to make something like a catamaran. Crew members slept in the starboard (right) pontoon, nicknamed the "tube of doom"; at least, on most cruises they did. Sleep was difficult on Ballard's trips, however, because he used the ship for seismic research. In this type of research, sounds—very loud sounds—were bounced off the ocean bottom, essentially creating artificial earthquakes. The pattern of returning echoes, detected by an array of hydrophones dragged behind the ship, outlined the heights and depths of the sea floor.

Developed by Woods Hole Oceanographic Institution with funding from the Office of Naval Research, the submersible Alvin served marine science well for 40 years (1964–2004). Alvin is shown here off Miami, Florida, in about 1967. Ballard, who first rode in Alvin in 1971, went on to make more dives in the small craft than any other scientist. He was one of Alvin's most tireless advocates in the late 1960s and 1970s, but later he decided that robot vehicles controlled from a surface ship were safer and more efficient tools for exploring the deep sea. (Woods Hole Oceanographic Institution Archives)

Lulu had not been employed for seismic studies before, and its crew members were not used to being rocked by ear-shattering explosions from a giant air gun that went off every 20 seconds, day and night. A burly, drunken sailor became so annoyed by the racket one night that he tried to attack Ballard with a knife. Fortunately, the ship's chief bo'sun had been watching for trouble and disarmed the man before he could strike.

Alvin returned to service in spring 1971, and Ballard finally made his first dive in the submersible on July 18. After scrambling aboard the swaying craft, awash in a choppy sea, he crouched beneath its instrument racks and tried to stay out of the way as the pilot and copilot took the tiny sub down. Since this was a shallow dive, the submersible reached the seafloor in a mere 10 minutes.

Positioning it on a rock outcrop so that the coring drill attached to its manipulator arm could dig out the samples Ballard needed proved to be a challenge, however. The vibration of the drill made *Alvin* swing back and forth like a pendulum, and that motion, in turn, usually caused the drill bit to jam. Obtaining two usable samples took almost five hours.

Ballard made 24 dives during the next year and a half—more than any other scientist had made in *Alvin* up to that time. He obtained usable rock samples on almost every one. By contrast, he almost never succeeded in gathering good samples by dredging from a surface ship, which he tried for comparison purposes. His success convinced him that he was right in believing that submersibles should be used mostly for precisely targeted missions like the ones he was carrying out.

An Exciting Opportunity

In late 1971, while Ballard was still busy with his thesis research, he learned about an exciting possible opportunity for *Alvin*. It, too, would be a test of the plate tectonics theory, but it would be far more extensive and dramatic than his project. Xavier Le Pichon (1937–), a French marine geophysicist, wrote to K. O. Emery (1914–98) at WHOI, proposing a combined French and U.S. exploration of the rift valley that ran down the center of the Mid-Atlantic Ridge, a range of undersea mountains in the middle of the Atlantic Ocean. According to the theory of seafloor spreading, an important part of plate tectonics, this valley should be one of the places where forces in the mantle, the layer underlying Earth's crust, split the crust apart and pushed it away on either side, forming the ridge. Magma, or molten rock from the mantle, gushed up into the cracks, encountered the chilly water of the deep sea, and hardened into a type of rock called basalt, which was similar to the lava spewed out by volcanic eruptions on land.

Le Pichon, backed by the French government's *Centre National pour l'Exploitation des Océans* (CNEXO), was thinking about using submersibles to obtain a firsthand view of a section of the valley, map it in detail, and sample its rocks. Such research could provide final confirmation of the seafloor-spreading theory and perhaps reveal new information about the way the Earth's crust was created. He wanted to know Emery's opinion of the idea, and Emery in turn told Ballard to prepare a reply.

Ballard believed that *Alvin* could do the U.S. part of the job. A problem existed, however: The rift valley lay 9,000 feet (2,743 m) beneath the sea, and *Alvin* was allowed to dive only to 6,000 feet (1,829 m). Fortunately, a solution seemed to be on the way. In 1973, *Alvin*'s steel alloy personnel sphere was scheduled to be replaced by one made of titanium, a metal even better able to withstand the tremendous pressure of the depths than steel was. The new sphere was still undergoing tests when WHOI received Le Pichon's letter, but Ballard felt sure that once the sphere was installed, the sub could dive to the required depth.

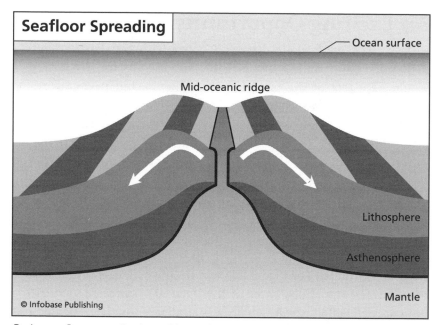

During seafloor spreading in a mid-oceanic ridge, molten rock from the Earth's mantle is forced upward to the surface of the crust at vents or fissures in the rift valley within the ridge. When the hot liquid rock contacts the icy ocean water, the rock solidifies, pushing away the seafloor on either side of it. As the seafloor moves away from the valley, it forms the mountains of the ridge. "Stripes" of normal and reversed magnetism, representing changes in the Earth's magnetic field over time, were found around mid-oceanic ridges and provided evidence to support the theory of seafloor spreading.

This technical problem was not the only challenge that *Alvin* and Ballard faced. The National Science Foundation supported the French proposal to send an international expedition to the Mid-Atlantic Ridge, but the role of submersibles in the project was anything but settled. Most older marine geologists and geophysicists were used to techniques carried out on surface ships, such as seismology, and considered the little vessels to be of unproven value at best. To win permission for *Alvin* to take part in the French-U.S. project, Ballard knew he would have to persuade the country's most powerful earth scientists that submersibles could successfully explore the ridge.

Titanium Paper Clips

On January 25, 1972, Robert Ballard faced 40 eminent scientists in a lecture hall at Princeton University, preparing to give a speech as part of a symposium on the ridge project. Understandably, he was more than a little nervous: He was the youngest person in the room, and he was not yet a Ph.D. Nonetheless, as he reminded himself, he had had more experience in field mapping with a submersible than anyone else present.

Ballard proceeded to describe his success in using *Alvin* to observe, map, and sample undersea rock formations. By the end of his speech, however, many faces in the audience still wore skeptical expressions. "Name one significant scientific paper in which a submersible has made a contribution," Frank Press, then the head of the Massachusetts Institute of Technology's (MIT) department of geology and geophysics, demanded.

Ballard felt trapped by circular logic. It was true that submersibles had not yet taken part in any significant published scientific work. However, he felt that this was so only because no scientist had dared to take such a craft on a major expedition whose results had been published. (His own research had not yet seen print.) Luckily for Ballard, geophysicist Bruce Luyendyk spoke up on his behalf and pointed this out.

Ballard's enthusiasm eventually carried the day: The symposium's final report recommended that surface surveys of the ridge be followed up with detailed investigations "using the capabilities of deep-towed vehicles and submersibles." Some of the meeting's members made it clear that they still had their doubts, however. One was the formidable Maurice ("Doc") Ewing (1906–74), head of Columbia University's Lamont-Doherty Earth Observatory. "Ballard, you may get a chance to try with your little submarine," Ewing growled at dinner that night. "But if you fail, we'll melt that submersible down into titanium paper clips."

By this time, Ballard had completed his research and was writing his doctoral dissertation. He used his seismic soundings and rock samples, whose age he could determine by measuring the breakdown of radioactive materials in them, to map the history of the underwater part of the Newark Formation. He showed that the New England coast began to form 200 million years ago, just when the plate tectonics theory said that North America and Africa were separating.

Project FAMOUS Begins

The exploration of the Mid-Atlantic Ridge, by then named Project FAMOUS (French-American Mid-Ocean Undersea Study), began in 1973. James Heirtzler, head of WHOI's department of marine geology and geophysics, was in charge of the U.S. part of the program. Ballard worked with him and the French scientists to plan the project's course of action. They focused on an area of the ridge's rift valley about 60 miles (97 km) square, some 400 miles (644 km) southwest of the island of San Miguel in the Azores. The valley floor at that spot was deeper than either *Alvin* or the other small submersible in the group, the French *Cyana* (designed by famed ocean explorer Jacques Cousteau [1910–77], who had originally called it the Diving Saucer), had ever dived.

FAMOUS's activities in 1973 consisted mainly of survey work. Planes carrying magnetic sensors mapped the site to see whether it would reveal the striped pattern of magnetism that had provided some of the most convincing evidence for seafloor spreading in the late 1960s. Seismometers on surface ships recorded dozens of small earthquakes, which confirmed that the planet's crust was moving near the site. Ballard persuaded the navy to map the area with an improved form of sonar (SOund Navigation and Ranging, a technology that uses sound echoes to locate objects and map terrain under water) that was still classified, or secret, and allow the FAMOUS team to use the maps. WHOI scientists took thousands of underwater photographs with ANGUS (Acoustically Navigated Geological Undersea Surveyor), a steel sled carrying three black-and-white cameras that was lowered on a cable from a surface ship and dragged around the site. Ballard and a team of WHOI engineers had developed ANGUS especially for use during FAMOUS.

The French team also made a few preliminary dives in the third deep-sea craft that would take part in the main expedition, the French navy bathyscaphe *Archimède*. *Archimède* was the largest deep-diving submersible in the world at the time. On August 5, 1973, Ballard went on the second *Archimède* dive and experienced a little more excitement than he would have liked. A short circuit started a small electrical fire, and the cumbersome craft had to resurface quickly when its passenger sphere filled with smoke.

As if the smoke and fire were not terrifying enough, Ballard put on his emergency oxygen mask during the ascent and found that the mask was not providing air. When he tried to tear the mask off his face, the bathyscaphe pilot jammed it back on, thinking that Ballard was having a panic attack. Ballard finally communicated his problem by drawing his finger across his throat, a universal diver's signal for "no air." The apologetic pilot then realized that he had not turned on the oxygen supply to Ballard's mask. Once this was done, Ballard could breathe again. He was proud to be the first U.S. scientist and the second scientist (after Le Pichon, who had been in *Archimède* on its first dive) to see the bizarre landscape of the undersea ridge for himself, but this dive left him less than impressed with bathyscaphes.

An Amazing Valley

In *Explorations*, Ballard called the first half of 1974 "the busiest months of my life." He obtained his Ph.D. degree on June 5, the day before the WHOI research ship *Knorr*, towing *Lulu* with *Alvin* aboard, set sail for the Project FAMOUS dive site. He also was promoted to assistant scientist in geology and geophysics at WHOI at about this time.

Robert Ballard helped to organize Project FAMOUS (French-American Mid-Ocean Undersea Study), which used both surface ships and submersibles to explore a rift valley in the Mid-Atlantic Ridge in 1973 and 1974. Ballard, shown here on the Woods Hole Oceanographic Institution surface vessel Knorr during the project, made several dives in Alvin to see the valley for himself. (Emory Kristoff/National Geographic Image Collection)

Ballard shared *Knorr* with 23 other scientists and technicians, as well as with Walter Sullivan, a reporter from the *New York Times*, and Emory Kristof, a photographer from the National Geographic Society. Ballard had invited these media representatives to attend and document the expedition, feeling that the publicity would benefit WHOI, *Alvin*, and marine science in general. He himself wrote one of the two articles about Project FAMOUS that appeared, illustrated with Kristof's photographs, in the May 1975 *National Geographic*. (James Heirtzler wrote the other.) Ballard's interest in popular (as opposed to scientific) writing in general, and his association with *National Geographic* in particular, would continue throughout his career.

The site on which the three submersibles dived during the main part of Project FAMOUS in summer 1974 was 20 miles (32 km) long and a half-mile to two miles (0.8 to 3 km) wide. Two volcanoes, dubbed Mount Venus and Mount Pluto, marked the ends of the site. The French explored the area around Mount Venus, while U.S. scientists dove around Mount Pluto.

Alvin carried a variety of new equipment on its descents, ranging from a sophisticated navigation system to a homemade water sampler made from the suction cups of two toilet plungers. The navigation system, combined with the extremely accurate maps prepared from the previous year's surveys, helped scientists in the submersible pinpoint exactly where they were when they collected each sample of rock, water, or other material. A tube in the center of the water sampler collected the sample, after which a trigger attached to the device made the cups slap together to close off and protect the tube.

Ballard made his first Project FAMOUS dive in *Alvin* on July 1, 1974. As he reported in *National Geographic,* the rift valley that he beheld was an amazing sight. A deep trough ran down its center, surrounded by seafloor that was split by many small cracks and crevasses. Instead of spewing out as in volcanic eruptions on land, lava apparently oozed up through these tiny fissures as the movement of the crustal plates pulled the seafloor apart. The seawater cooled and hardened the lava so quickly that a thin layer of pure glass formed on the outside of each rock. The lava was shiny and black, too new to have acquired the gray coating of sediment that covered the older deposits on the sides of the valley. It took on fantastic shapes that the scientists delighted in naming: pillow, toothpaste, haystack, broken egg, and more. Jim Moore of the U.S. Geological Survey, one of the scientists on the dives, called the site "a geologist's dream."

Two weeks later, a much larger fissure provided the project's most frightening moment for the *Alvin* team. Ballard was not in the submersible during this dive but rather was taking his turn as surface navigator, tracking the sub's progress from the control room on *Lulu.* At one point, he noticed that *Alvin* had not moved for quite a while. He told the ship's pilot, Jack Donnelly, "Better get under way. Mission time is running out."

"We're trying," Donnelly replied tensely. "We don't seem to be able to rise." He explained that the two geologists aboard *Alvin* had spotted the fissure, and Donnelly had thought it looked big enough to hold the submersible. He therefore took the ship down to investigate. Unfortunately, none of the three men noticed that while they cruised along comfortably below, the walls of the fissure were narrowing at the top. By the time they realized the problem, *Alvin* was stuck. More than two hours passed before Donnelly, working with the advice of senior pilot Val Wilson on the surface, managed to back the submersible out of its trap. Donnelly said the experience had been "like backing a Cadillac out of a VW parking space."

Alvin made 18 dives in 23 days, ending on August 16. The French made a total of 27 dives in *Archimède* and *Cyana* during the same period. The submersibles and surface ships together took more than 100,000 photographs of the ridge and valley and gathered a ton and a half of geological samples. The magnetic, geochemical, gravitational, and seismic studies made during the project showed clear, direct proof that the seafloor spreading theory was correct and provided the most detailed and comprehensive investigation of a spreading center made up to that time. Not least, Project FAMOUS provided an excellent example of international cooperation and, to Ballard's delight, demonstrated just how useful small submersibles could be in undersea research. Maurice Ewing, it seemed, would have to do without his titanium paper clips.

Undersea Gardens
and Black Smokers

Robert Ballard led his first large research expedition in 1976, the same year he was promoted to associate scientist at WHOI. By this time, he was considered the institute's expert on submersibles, since he had made more dives in *Alvin* than any other scientist. His expedition took the little sub to the Cayman Trough, just south of Cuba. This undersea trench, dropping to 23,000 feet (7,010 m) below the Caribbean and stretching 930 miles (1,497 km) into the Atlantic Ocean from Central America, marks the gap between the American and Caribbean plates. Geologists were interested in the trough because it creates a deep slice through the Earth's crust, revealing layers of rock clear down to the mantle. Indeed, one of *Alvin*'s dives during Ballard's expedition took the submersible to its new lower limit of 12,000 feet (3,658 m) and collected a dark rock with a soft, flaky surface that may have come from the mantle itself.

In addition to examining and sampling the rocks in the walls of the trench, the expedition photographed the seafloor at the trough's bottom with ANGUS. The little sled, much improved since its days on Project FAMOUS, now sported sensitive color cameras that had replaced its black-and-white ones. It descended as low as 20,000 feet (6,096 m), far deeper than *Alvin* could go.

Ballard continued his expedition in 1977 with dives in the U.S. navy bathyscaphe *Trieste II* to collect fresh lava from the trench floor. The first two dives were uneventful, but during the third, the front of the clumsy craft crashed into the cliff wall and ruptured some of its flotation tanks. Ballard feared that without its full stock of buoyant gasoline, the bathyscaphe might not be able to return to the surface. Fortunately, lightening the vessel by dumping the iron pellets that it carried as ballast, combined with the lift from the remaining gasoline, rescued the *Trieste II*. At the end of its nerve-wrackingly slow ascent, however, Ballard promised himself that he would never dive in a bathyscaphe again.

Looking for Undersea Geysers

Ballard made a far more important series of dives during a different research trip in February and March 1977. He was this expedition's technical chief, in charge especially of its work with ANGUS. The trip went to the Galápagos Rift, a part of the Mid-Ocean Ridge's rift valley that ran under the Pacific about 200 miles (322 km) from the Galápagos Islands. The strange animal life of these islands, located near Ecuador, had inspired Charles Darwin (1809–82) to propose his theory of evolution by natural selection in the mid-19th century.

The expedition, which included 51 scientists and technicians from several institutions, was intended to study the flow of heat in the rift valley. WHOI geophysicist Richard von Herzen, the group's chief scientist, specialized in this subject. He had predicted the changes in temperature that should occur as hot rock moved up from the mantle in such valleys and cooled when it spread out toward the mid-ocean ridge on either side. Temperature data gathered during Project FAMOUS fitted his predictions for the ridges, but the temperature on the valley floor proved to be much lower than von Herzen expected.

One possible explanation for this unusual pattern was a process called hydrothermalism. In hydrothermal circulation, cold seawater sinks into fissures in the ocean floor, is heated by the magma beneath, and rises back up in the deep-sea equivalent of hot springs or geysers on land. This heat exchange process uses up some heat energy, and that loss could explain the lower temperatures that the FAMOUS scientists had observed.

The scientists did not find any hot springs during FAMOUS, but von Herzen thought this might be because the seafloor was spreading apart fairly slowly—by just an inch (2.5 cm) a year—at the Atlantic site. The plates near the Galápagos Rift, part of the East Pacific Rise, were moving much faster, some 2–7 inches (6–18 cm) a year. That meant that more molten rock, and therefore more heat, would rise to the surface there. Hydrothermal effects thus should be easier to detect. The main purpose of the 1977 research trip, called the Galápagos Hydrothermal Expedition, was to look for such effects.

Some signs of them had already been found. The year before, scientists from the Scripps Institution of Oceanography had visited the area and recorded water and mud temperatures slightly higher than expected. They had also dragged their *Deep Tow* probe, a device somewhat similar to ANGUS but more complex and fragile, along the rift and photographed large mounds of what might be minerals deposited by the proposed hot springs, or hydrothermal vents. One *Deep Tow* photograph showed a heap of shells that appeared to belong to clams. The photo also included a beer bottle, so the Scripps researchers assumed that both bottle and clam shells were garbage that a passing ship had tossed overboard. As a joke, they named the site "Clambake."

A Bizarre Landscape

Ballard and the other scientists on the WHOI expedition traveled to the Galápagos on the institution's research ship *Knorr*. They began their research by photographing the seafloor with ANGUS, which *Knorr* towed as it steamed back and forth along the rift. ANGUS was simple—some of the crew members called it the "dope on a rope"—but reliable; it had survived many collisions with undersea cliffs and even an accident in the Cayman Trough in 1976 that had threatened to snap its cable, losing it in the depths forever. (After that incident, someone had scrawled on the camera sled's side, "Takes a licking and keeps on clicking.") Its thousands of color photographs gave the researchers on *Knorr* a clear look at the rift valley's terrain.

On February 15, 1977, during ANGUS's first pass across the site, sensors on the sled—which now included a thermistor, a device that could detect changes in temperature—reported a sudden temperature rise at a spot about 1.5 miles (2.5 km) below the surface. To the researchers' surprise, the ANGUS photograph taken at that location, like the one the Scripps scientists had mentioned, showed clams. These clams, however, were clearly living, not a heap of discarded shells. They were also huge—as big as dinner plates. A few kinds of animals were able to survive in the barren desert of the deep sea by eating the remains of shallow-water organisms and other bits of organic matter that drifted down as "marine snow," but clams were not known to be among them. What could the mollusks be using for food?

The clams were only the first of the puzzles that met the increasingly amazed scientists' eyes. The water at that depth was usually clear, but in the area of higher temperature it was filled with swirling, milky clouds. After some of the researchers descended in *Alvin* to look more closely at these clouds, they concluded that the floating matter was particles of minerals, especially manganese, which gave the clouds a sky-blue color. Such mineral plumes were a sure sign of a hydrothermal vent. John Edmond, a geochemist with the expedition, reported later that the water shimmered in *Alvin*'s headlights "like the air above a hot pavement."

The scientists found a second hydrothermal vent later in the same dive. They brought up samples of the organisms that clustered around both vents, including a clam, several dark-brown mussels, and a clump of rock coated with living slime. In a second dive on the same site—which, following the Scripps scientists' example, they named Clambake I—they retrieved samples of the vent water as well.

The researchers uncovered the first clue to the mystery of the vent creatures' food source when they smelled the water samples. As soon as the sample containers were opened on *Knorr*'s deck, the air filled with the rotten-egg reek of hydrogen sulfide gas. The scientists guessed that this compound had been created from dissolved sulfates in the seawater by the magma's heat during the hydrothermal process and then had been carried back up into the sea when the heated water rose through the vents.

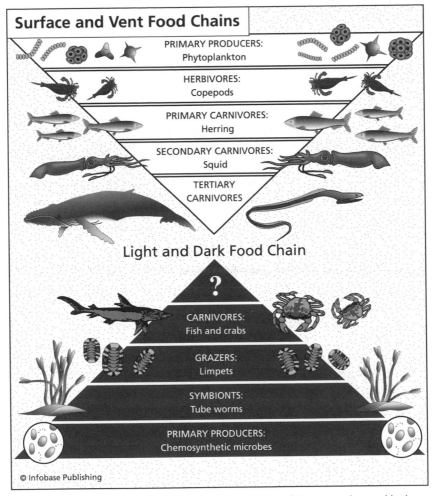

This diagram contrasts the food chains near the surface of the sea and around hydro-thermal vents. In both cases, the primary producers are living things that can make their own food: phytoplankton (tiny, floating plants and plantlike microorganisms) near the surface and chemosynthetic (sulfur-digesting) microbes at the vents. The second layer of the chain at the surface is herbivores such as copepods (small shrimplike animals) which eat the phytoplankton; at the vents, it is animals such as tube worms which obtain their food from chemosynthetic bacteria living inside their bodies. In turn, primary carnivores at the surface eat the herbivores, while grazers at the vents scrape the bacteria and other minute creatures from the vent surfaces. Secondary carnivores eat the smaller primary carnivores and in turn are eaten by tertiary carnivores. At the vents, fish and crabs eat smaller animals that graze on the bacteria.

The vent animals that *Alvin* brought to the surface also smelled strongly of hydrogen sulfide. This substance is poisonous to most living things, but John Edmond pointed out that some swamp-dwelling bacteria can combine hydrogen sulfide with oxygen and obtain energy from the reaction in a process called chemosynthesis. If bacteria near the hydrothermal vents could also gain energy from

Garden of Eden

In *Explorations,* Robert Ballard described his first view of the amazing life that clustered around the Galápagos Rift's hydrothermal vents as follows:

> *My face was pressed to [Alvin's] portside view port. . . . Suddenly, our floodlights revealed a swaying field of orangish pink [animals that looked like] dandelions, their puffy heads pulsing with fine webs of filaments in response to Alvin's pressure wave. The lumped mounds of pillow lava were thick with jutting chalk white clam shells, some of them a foot in length. In a few isolated clusters, cocoa brown mussels had formed subcolonies.*

Victoria Kaharl expanded on this description in *Water Baby,* her history of *Alvin.* Speaking of the submersible's first dive to the "Clambake I" site, she wrote the following:

> *There were huge clamshells, stark white against the black elephant-skin basalt; brown mussels; a big bright red shrimp; a couple of white crabs scampering over the basalt; white squat lobsters; a brittlestar; a large pale [sea] anemone. . . . A many-legged creature pumped itself out of sight. Something sticking out of the bottom. Coral? A pretty little pale orange ball that looked like a dandelion gone to seed. Rocks covered in white streaks, what looked like pigeon droppings. Worms? A white crab climbed onto Alvin's pink milk crate and fell off. The water got foggy. Six of those white crabs. A whole cluster of those little peach-colored puffballs. And for as far as they could see, more clams and mussels—or were they oysters?—tucked in among the bulbous, black basalt.*

No wonder an awed John Edmond later commented, "This is what it must have been like sailing with Columbus."

hydrogen sulfide through chemosynthesis, the clams and other living things around the vents might form a food chain with the bacteria at its base. Later research showed that this idea was correct. The vent communities were the first ecosystem ever discovered that did not depend on plants' ability to capture energy from the Sun through photosynthesis.

Unique Ecosystems

Ballard and the other scientists explored four more hydrothermal vent communities during the 1977 expedition. Each was a unique oasis of incredible life, extending 13 to 16 feet (4 to 5 m) from the vent that provided its energy. Not only clams but also crabs, mussels, shrimp, and other living things swarmed around the vents. Most were of familiar types, although the species were new. Some of the animals, however, might as well have come from another planet. Among these were organisms that looked like fuzzy pink dandelions, which proved to be related to jellyfish, and worms that waved red plumes from the tops of white tubes like a forest of bloody-headed snakes. The scientists also saw around the vents mats of organic material that they suspected were colonies of the sulfur-eating bacteria. One of the scientists, Jack Corliss of Oregon State University, even speculated that life on Earth might have begun around hydrothermal vents like these, an idea that some scientists still entertain.

Because the Galápagos Hydrothermal Expedition had expected to focus on geology, no biologists were on board, and *Knorr* did not carry equipment for collecting and preserving biological specimens. The scientists knew, however, that marine biologists would be fascinated by the vent animals and would want to see as many samples of them as possible. The group therefore pressed into action every type of container and preservative they could find—including, Ballard wrote in *Explorations,* "several cases of good Russian vodka."

Discovery of the hydrothermal vents alone would have made the Galápagos cruise a historic event in marine science. "Vents like these must be pushing the entire ocean through them every four or five million years," John Edmond speculated. (Later researchers confirmed this idea, though they increased the time span for the circulation to about 10 million years.) The vents provided an important new source for minerals in the ocean, which until then had been thought to come only from river runoff.

The finding of the bizarre communities of living things around the vents, however, was even more important. An article in the July 2000 issue of *American Scientist* called it "the most important discovery in marine biology in 200 years." Robert Ballard wrote in *Explorations,* "We had discovered what amounted to an entire separate branch of evolution down in those dark lava mounds, a virtual new planet for biologists to explore."

Biologists eager to see this "new planet" with their own eyes crowded onto a second expedition to the Galápagos Rift two years later. In this 1979 journey, as on the 1977 one, Robert Ballard headed the team that handled ANGUS's reconnaissance photography.

The scientists gave the hydrothermal oases fanciful names such as "The Garden of Eden" and "The Rose Garden." Unloading specimens of vent life on *Knorr*'s deck each day "was like a child's Christmas morning," Victoria Kaharl wrote in *Water Baby: The Story of* Alvin. "Presents" in the haul included such bizarre creatures as a small crustacean that had teeth instead of eyes on the tips of its eyestalks; it probably used the teeth to scrape bacteria from rocks and mussel shells. The scientist who described it "knew of no other animal that gathered lunch with its eyes," Kaharl reported.

The researchers found many vent species that, like the clams seen in 1977, were giants compared to known types of similar animals—or even animals that had been observed on the earlier trip. For instance, they saw tube worms 12 feet (3.6 m) high, tremendous compared to the 18-inch (46-cm) worms that the first expedition had reported. They also discovered about 200 different species of sulfur-eating bacteria, clustering in mats in and around the vents and floating out in clumps to feed the organisms around them. Some of the cloudiness of the water around the vents was due to these bacteria.

Some of the vent animals, including the plate-sized clams, had bright red flesh, "like the face of a freshly cut steak," as Ballard put it in *Explorations.* Biologists found that the red came from hemoglobin, the substance that makes human blood red and carries oxygen through the body. Even though the vent creatures depended on

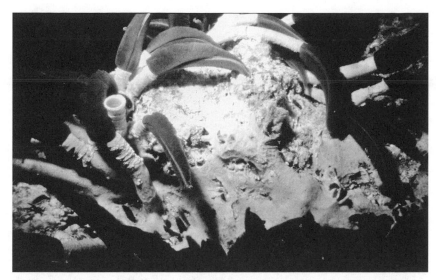

Giant tube worms were among the strangest of the creatures that Robert Ballard and other scientists found living around hydrothermal vents in the late 1970s. The worms, which lack a digestive system, survive on nutrients made by sulfur-digesting bacteria in their bodies. The tube worms shown here, a species called Riftia pachyptila, are found around vents in the East Pacific Rise. (OAR/National Undersea Research Program [NURP]; College of William and Mary)

hydrogen sulfide, they also had to obtain small amounts of oxygen from the water, and the scientists suspected that the extra hemoglobin helped the animals survive at times when outpourings from the vents made the oxygen content of the seawater unusually low.

The gigantic tubeworms proved to be stranger still. They were so different from all other animals that biologists placed them in a new phylum. (As Robert Kunzig wrote in *Mapping the Deep: The Extraordinary Story of Ocean Science,* "To say that [this kind of animal] belongs to a new phylum is to say that it has less in common with everything else that lives in the sea than fish or sea squirts [a primitive animal that has a spinal cord but no backbone] do with us.") The worms had no mouths or digestive tracts, so at first no one could guess how they obtained food. A Harvard marine biologist, Colleen Cavenaugh, solved this puzzle in 1981 by showing that bacteria able to metabolize hydrogen sulfide live inside the worms' bodies. With the help of oxygen absorbed from the water through the worms' tentacles, the bacteria make enough nutrients to feed the worms as well as themselves. Hemoglobin in the tubeworms' red plumes carries oxygen and hydrogen sulfide from the water to the bacteria. Some of the other vent animals also proved to obtain their nourishment from bacteria inside their bodies.

Black Smokers

In February 1978, between his two trips to the Galápagos, Robert Ballard took part in a different research project that also made spectacular discoveries. Some of the French scientists from CNEXO with whom Ballard had worked on Project FAMOUS led this expedition. Like the hydrothermal team, the French researchers wanted to study a portion of the Mid-Ocean Ridge where plates were moving apart faster than the ones at the FAMOUS site, so they went to the East Pacific Rise. They chose a location about 100 miles (161 km) south of the southern tip of Baja California, the slender peninsula belonging to Mexico that extends from the southern part of the state. They called the expedition RITA after the first two letters of Rivera and Tamayo, two earthquake faults that marked the boundaries of the area that they planned to explore.

In 1979, Ballard and other scientists discovered a type of hydrothermal vent called a black smoker, shown here. Black smokers spew out seawater that, heated by the molten layer below Earth's crust, can be hot enough to melt lead. Dissolved minerals in the water make it look black. When contact with the chilly ocean cools the water from the vents, the minerals are deposited on their sides to form chimneys. (OAR/National Undersea Research Program [NURP]; NOAA)

The team worked from *Le Suroit,* a French research ship, and brought the submersible *Cyana,* but Ballard was disappointed to learn that they had no tool like ANGUS to survey the site and help them choose the spots for their dives.

Some of the most unusual rock formations that the French team saw during the first year of RITA were flat "lakes" of hardened lava from which rose tall towers, also made of lava. ANGUS had photographed similar formations near the Galápagos Rift during Ballard's 1977 expedition. Some of the scientists on that expedition thought that the tubelike towers might have formed when jets of seawater shot up through fissures from which magma had recently poured, instantly cooling and hardening the outermost layer of the molten lava. The rest of the lava eventually drained away, leaving the hardened part behind. Ballard observed the towers closely in *Cyana* and even took a sample from one. He found that the towers were hollow, just as he and the others had suspected.

Accompanied by a team from WHOI as well as *Alvin* and *Lulu,* Ballard rejoined RITA after he returned from the 1979 dive on the Galápagos Rift. When Ballard and others rode down to examine the undersea towers in *Alvin,* they found to their amazement that one of the hollow structures was belching out fountains of what looked like black smoke. Smoke could not exist under water, of course, so the scientists assumed that sulfides and other dissolved minerals made the water dark.

Smoke, however, would have been appropriate—because the vent certainly contained the underwater equivalent of fire. *Alvin*'s temperature probe registered 91° F (32°C) when the scientists inserted it in the outer part of the fountain. That was lower than a human's body temperature, but it was far warmer than anything recorded from the hydrothermal vents of the Galápagos Rift. When *Alvin* was hauled back aboard *Lulu* that evening, furthermore, the researchers saw with a shock that the plastic tip of the temperature probe had melted. On a return dive with a more heat-resistant probe the following day, the scientists wisely tested the water pouring out of the lava chimney before going closer. It was an amazing 662° F (350°C)—hot enough to have melted parts of the submersible itself. "We were less than 10 feet [3 m] away from death and destruction," Ballard wrote later. Jean Francheteau, the leader of the French part of the expedition, summed up the group's feelings when he said of the chimneys, "They seem connected to hell itself."

Ballard called the chimneys "black smokers," a term that other scientists also came to use. Some of the smokers were 30 feet (9 m) tall. They proved to be made largely of a mineral called sphalerite, a form of zinc sulfide. The "smoke" clouds, like the water pouring from the quieter vents in the Galápagos Rift, contained large quantities of hydrogen sulfide and other sulfur compounds. The clouds were also rich in metals such as zinc, iron, and copper. Solid deposits of metal sulfides sometimes formed on the sides of the smoker chimneys, painting the lava with streaks of yellow, ocher, and reddish brown. Most black smokers had their own versions of the giant clams, tube-worms, and other unique animals found around hydrothermal vents. Black smokers have since been found at seafloor spreading sites all over the world.

Telepresence

Even though Robert Ballard and other scientists had made spectacular discoveries in *Alvin,* Ballard was beginning to rethink his early enthusiasm for direct human exploration of the deep sea. He decided that what he called "telepresence"—exploration through robot devices that could be controlled from a surface ship—would be safer, cheaper, and more effective. He later defined telepresence as "being able to project your spirit to the bottom, your eyes, your mind, and being able to leave your body behind."

In 1980, the same year he was awarded tenure (a permanent position) at WHOI, Ballard took time off from Woods Hole to develop his ideas about telepresence and remotely operated vehicles, or ROVs, during a sabbatical year at Stanford University in northern California. Unlike manned submersibles, which had to surface after a few hours to recharge their batteries, ROVs could remain underwater for days or even weeks at a time. The devices Ballard envisioned would be much more sophisticated than sturdy but simple ANGUS, the "dope on a rope." ANGUS took still photos on film that had to be developed after the sled was retrieved. Ballard's new ROVs, by contrast, would be able to send color photos and video images to their controllers in real time. Through television links and computer satellites, they could also share their images with others—perhaps millions of others—in distant parts of the world.

Ballard planned a system with two parts, to which he gave names from an ancient Greek myth about treasure hunters who set out in a ship to look for a legendary "golden fleece." His larger device would be *Argo,* the name of the ship in the story, and his smaller robot would be *Jason,* the name of the group's leader. *Argo,* the improved version of ANGUS, would be lowered from a surface ship. *Jason,* the more maneuverable robot, would ride down with *Argo* and then be released to take a closer look at whatever its handlers found interesting. As Ballard wrote in an article in the December 1986 *National Geographic,* "*Argo* was to be the eyes of the system and *Jason* the hands." *Jason* would be connected to *Argo* by a fiber-optic cable through which pictures could be transmitted. Both devices would send color video to the mother ship, where scientists in a control room would watch it and direct the robots interactively, as if they were playing a video game.

As always, Ballard had to find financial support before he could turn his ideas about *Argo* and *Jason* into reality. A chance to speak to top-ranking navy officials about future trends in submarine warfare in summer 1982 gave him the opportunity he sought. He stated that the future was likely to belong to small, maneuverable combat submarines like the navy's miniature nuclear submarine *NR-1.* Instead of avoiding tricky terrain like the mid-ocean ridges and the twisting canyons that interlaced them, he said, such submarines could take advantage of the many hiding places that this kind of landscape offered. They could effectively block undersea "choke points" such as the Strait of Gibraltar and the entrances to the Sea of Japan. He went on to explain how the military could use his proposed *Argo-Jason* system in this new kind of submarine warfare. By the end of 1982, Ballard had persuaded the navy to fund the development of his imaging system.

Argo and *Jason*

Ballard created his robots in the Deep Submergence Laboratory at WHOI, which he had established in 1981 as an extension of his

ANGUS group. He began with *Argo,* which at first was not too different from ANGUS. Standard coaxial cable, not the fiber-optic cable that Ballard hoped to use in later models, connected it to its mother ship. Its video cameras were black-and-white, not color.

The Sinking of *Titanic:* A Night to Remember

At the time it was launched on May 31, 1911, RMS *Titanic* was the largest and probably the most luxurious passenger steamship in the world. (RMS stands for "Royal Mail Steamer," a designation the ship was given because it carried mail, even though mail transport was not its chief function.) Measuring 883 feet (269 m) long by 93 feet (28 m) wide, *Titanic* potentially could carry 3,547 passengers and crew. It featured a swimming pool, a gym, two libraries, and salons decorated with expensive wood paneling. An advertisement of the time stated that the beautiful ship was "designed to be unsinkable."

Titanic left New York City for Southampton, England, on April 10, 1912—its first, or maiden, voyage. Some of the wealthiest and most famous people in the world slept in its first-class staterooms. On the night of April 14, it was on its way back to New York, traveling through the chilly waters of the Atlantic south of eastern Canada. In spite of reports that other ships had sighted icebergs in the area, *Titanic*'s captain, Edward J. Smith, kept the liner moving at a relatively high rate of speed.

At 11:40 P.M., the lookouts in *Titanic*'s crow's nest, high on the mast, spotted an iceberg directly in front of the vessel. They rang the ship's bell three times and shouted "Iceberg, right ahead!" into the telephone that connected them to the bridge, the ship's command center. The men there tried to turn the vessel, but the iceberg scraped along its side, tearing open five of its watertight compartments. It could have stayed afloat with four compartments flooded but not five.

Titanic's crew began to launch lifeboats at 12:27 A.M., but tragically the ship did not carry enough boats to hold all of its passengers and staff. The vessel also telegraphed calls for help and fired distress rockets. Other ships in the area, however, either were too far away or did not heed the signals. The closest ship, SS *Californian,* did not receive the messages because its telegraph operator had gone to bed for the night.

Of the 704 people who survived the disaster, 21 were still alive at the time Robert Ballard searched for *Titanic.* One was Ruth Becker

It was linked to a powerful sonar system on the surface ship and carried its own shorter-range but more sensitive sonar as well. Its cameras were so sensitive that they could take usable photographs in almost complete darkness.

In perhaps the most famous marine disaster of all time, the British luxury liner RMS Titanic sank in the North Atlantic on the night of April 14, 1912, after colliding with an iceberg. Partly because the ship did not carry enough lifeboats for its passengers, 1,522 people—about two-thirds of those on board—lost their lives. From boyhood on, Robert Ballard dreamed of discovering Titanic's wreckage. (HIP/Art Resource)

(later Blanchard), who had been 12 years old when she made that almost-fatal sea journey with her mother, her sister, and her brother (who also survived). "It was a very dark night," she told *Smithsonian* magazine writer Joy Waldron Murphy in 1986. "The ocean was as calm as a millpond. The ship's lights were on and the prow [front end of the ship] went in first. The stern [rear end] was upright for a moment or two. All of the people left on board started screaming, yelling, calling for help. I can still hear those screams."

The first *Jason,* a simplified model that Ballard called *Jason Jr.,* or *JJ* for short, could be linked by a second cable to either *Argo* or *Alvin.* Carrying lights and stereo video cameras, it could move under its own power, with guidance from the mother ship or from *Alvin,* to explore undersea geological features or the wreckage of sunken ships.

Once Ballard's ROVs were developed, the navy planned to test them by having them investigate the remains of *Thresher* and *Scorpion,* two of its submarines that had been lost to accidents. *Thresher,* the first of a new class of deep-diving nuclear attack submarines, sank 8,500 feet (2,591 m) down in the Atlantic on April 10, 1963, during its first sea tests. A small pipe had burst and shorted out its electrical system, after which its nuclear reactor shut down automatically as well. Without power, it quickly fell past its "crush depth" of 1,500 feet (457 m). Seawater under thousands of tons of pressure crumpled its hull like a tin can, killing its 129 crew members instantly. Thanks to earlier visits to the wreck site by *Alvin* and *Trieste II,* the navy was fairly sure of what had caused the disaster, but navy officials wanted Ballard to map and make a video record of the debris from the submarine in case it contained additional clues. *Scorpion* sank in the mid-Atlantic in 1968, probably because it was hit by one of its own homing torpedoes. In addition to learning more about both accidents, if possible, the navy wanted to verify that the submarines' nuclear reactors and *Scorpion's* nuclear torpedoes were not leaking radiation.

Ballard agreed to the navy's proposals since his funding depended on them, but investigating the two submarines was only the beginning of his plans for *Argo* and *Jason.* His real goal was far more exciting: to find and examine the wreckage of the most famous lost ship of all time, RMS *Titanic.* This British luxury liner, which its owners, the White Star Line, had proudly called unsinkable, had gone to the bottom of the North Atlantic after hitting an iceberg on April 14, 1912. About two-thirds of those on board were drowned or died of exposure in the chilly waters. The remains of *Titanic* were thought to be about 12,400 feet (3,780 m) below the sea's surface some 500 miles (805 km) south of the Canadian province of Newfoundland, but no one knew exactly where it lay. Ballard had dreamed of finding the famous wreck since he was a teenager, and he hoped that the technology he was now developing would allow him to fulfill that dream.

Following a Trail

By summer 1984, *Argo* was ready for testing on the *Thresher* wreck. (*Jason Jr.* was still on the drawing board.) Ballard began to map the submarine's debris field with the ROV on July 11. He was thrilled to view the sea bottom below *Argo* through the eyes of the sled's video cameras and to use that information to guide the vehicle, something he never could have done with ANGUS. He could see as well as if he were in *Alvin,* yet he sat safely and relatively comfortably in the control van on *Knorr'*s deck instead of being, as he put it in *The Discovery of the* Titanic, one of "three sardines in a spherical can" thousands of feet down in the lightless, high-pressure depths of the ocean. "We felt as if we were actually down there," he wrote in *Explorations.*

Ballard had little trouble finding pieces of lightweight debris that had been thrown out of *Thresher* when the submarine imploded, such as a boot and a rubber glove that had probably belonged to the engineering crew. At first, however, he could not spot the heavier debris that would mark the wreck site itself. He had expected the debris to lie in a circle around the site of the submarine's sinking, as happened with ships that sank in shallow water, but after a day of fruitless searching, he began to think that this assumption might be wrong. The heaviest debris, such as pieces of the submarine's armor plate, would have fallen straight to the bottom, but lighter-weight fragments could have been carried away by deep-water currents as they sank. If that had occurred, the debris would form a trail leading away from the site, beginning with the heaviest pieces and ending with the lightest ones. Shallow-water debris did not form such trails because it was exposed to currents only briefly before the objects reached the seafloor.

Ballard realized that the lightest pieces of debris *Argo* had spotted lay to the west of heavier ones. Acting on his new theory about the debris trail, he asked that *Knorr* be turned east. Sure enough, just as he had suspected, following the trail brought him quickly to what was left of *Thresher* itself. Even more important to him, Ballard recognized that his theory could be the breakthrough clue that would lead him to *Titanic.* He began to believe that, armed with this idea and his new remote-viewing technology, he would succeed in finding the famous wreck where so many others had failed.

A *Titanic* Discovery

By mid-August 1985, Robert Ballard was on his way to his goal at last. As *Knorr*, with *Argo* aboard, steamed toward the spot in the Atlantic where *Titanic* was thought to have gone down, Ballard had time to reflect on the long road he had traveled to reach this moment. He had been seeking funding actively to search for the lost liner since 1973. Gaining the navy's support for development of his *Argo-Jason* system had been a giant step forward, but he knew that the military had no interest in the *Titanic* project itself. Neither, he had learned, did the authorities at Woods Hole. The institute's current director, John Steele, did not feel that hunting for lost ships, however famous, was a legitimate part of marine science. If Ballard wanted to pursue that goal, Steele said, he would have to do it without the prestige of WHOI behind him.

Searching for the Wrong Reasons

Ballard had soon learned that some groups were quite eager to sponsor a search for *Titanic*—but, he felt, they wanted to do so for the wrong reasons. In 1977, a company called Big Events contacted him and offered to pay for the venture, but Ballard broke off negotiations with them when he learned that they planned to salvage debris from the wreck and sell it as souvenirs. He felt that such behavior would be an insult to the people who had died when the ship sank. His own intention was to map and photograph the wreckage extensively but otherwise leave it undisturbed.

Big Events did one good thing for Ballard, however: It introduced him to the *Titanic* Historical Society and that group's head, Bill Tantum. Tantum, often known as "Mr. *Titanic*," soon became Ballard's close friend. The society could not offer any funding, but Tantum was very enthusiastic about Ballard's project. He and the historical society greatly increased Ballard's knowledge of the ship, the people on it, and the events that had taken place on that terrible April night. Through them, Ballard learned to see *Titanic* as "a fascinating chapter in human history," as he put it in *The Discovery of the* Titanic, not just as a means to fulfill a youthful dream and prove his skill as an underwater explorer. He worked closely with Tantum until Tantum died from a stroke in 1980.

Big Events was by no means the only sponsor that wanted to find *Titanic* for what Ballard saw as less than noble motives. Another was an eccentric Texas oil millionaire named Jack Grimm, whom Ballard described in *The Discovery of the* Titanic as "a curious combination of hard-nosed business acumen and naïve schoolboy romanticism." Ballard refused to work with Grimm, but two other respected marine scientists, Fred Spiess and Bill Ryan, signed onto the oilman's project. If Spiess and Ryan had been allowed to control the search, Ballard thought they might well have beaten him to the ship. Grimm, however, overrode their decisions at key moments during the expeditions that the group made in 1980 and 1981, and partly as a result of his poor decisions, the missions failed. Grimm insisted in 1981 that he had found a propeller from *Titanic*, but the scientific community did not believe that his interpretation of a fuzzy video image was correct. An attempt to take a closer look at the supposed propeller in 1983 also produced nothing.

A Frustrating Start

Ballard finally obtained the help he needed for his *Titanic* mission from his old colleagues, the French. In 1984 he persuaded the Institut Français de Recherche pour l'Exploitation de la Mer (the French Research Institute for Exploitation of the Sea, or IFREMER), which had replaced CNEXO, that taking part in a joint project to locate *Titanic* would bring France the same kind of favorable publicity and access to new U.S. technology that Project FAMOUS had produced. Finding the renowned ship, he said, "would be the maritime [seagoing] equivalent of a successful moon landing." Eager to test a new sonar system that it had been developing, the French agency agreed to provide scientists and equipment for a preliminary search of the site. The leader of the French team at sea would be Jean-Louis Michel, a friend of Ballard's since the FAMOUS days.

Michel and the crew of the French research ship *Le Suroit* began their work at the *Titanic* site on July 5, 1985. Their new sonar system, SAR (*sonar acoustique remorqué*), could scan large areas at a time and produce computer-processed graphs so clear that they looked like black-and-white photos of the seafloor. To create these maps, the "bulbous red torpedo" (as Ballard described it) housing the sonar equipment had to be towed very precisely back and forth, always at the same height, in overlapping passes across the 100-square-mile (259-sq.-km) area that Ballard and Michel had agreed was the liner's most likely resting place. The researchers called this technique "mowing the lawn." In addition to sonar, the SAR device included a magnetometer, which would tell the scientists whether large objects that the sonar detected were made of metal, as of course the *Titanic*'s hull would be. If the French found anything interesting, Ballard would send *Argo* down to photograph it after he arrived.

By the time Ballard joined Michel on *Le Suroit* on July 22, the French had covered almost half of the search site without detecting any promising leads. The group began to fear that *Titanic* had been buried in undersea mudslides during the Grand Banks Earthquake in 1929. In case reports of the ship's position when it sank had been wrong, however, Ballard and Michel decided to expand their search area.

Le Suroit had "mowed the lawn" over more than about 80 percent of the original area and half of the expanded one—still without results—when the French ship had to depart for other projects on August 6. Ballard, Michel, and two other IFREMER scientists then flew to the Azores to join a crew from Ballard's Deep Submergence Laboratory aboard *Knorr* for the second half of the expedition.

Before they could go back to *Titanic,* Ballard had to fulfill the second half of his duty to the navy by mapping the site of the *Scorpion* wreck, which lay south of the Azores at a depth of 11,500 feet (3,505 m). Because this work was classified, Ballard could tell the French researchers only that he was testing some military equipment. They had to stay out of the control van on *Knorr*'s deck, from which *Argo* was managed, during that part of the expedition.

After four days, the naval representative aboard *Knorr* told Ballard that he could end the *Scorpion* survey. Ballard had permission to do whatever he wished with the rest of the three weeks of sea time that the navy had budgeted for field-testing *Argo.* Naturally, he ordered *Knorr* to head at once for the *Titanic* site.

Ballard's team of 25 scientists and technicians arrived at the site on August 24. They had only 12 days to hunt for the wreck before *Knorr,* too, would have to fulfill other commitments. To use that time efficiently, Ballard suggested that the group look for the field of debris around the wreck rather than for the ship itself, since that field was bound to be much larger than the hull of even such a gigantic vessel. He also felt that *Argo*'s photographic eyes would work better than sonar for detecting the field because even the most sensitive sonar would not show lightweight debris.

Before the search began, Ballard explained to Michel his new idea that the debris from a ship that sank in deep water would stream out like a comet's tail rather than spread in a circle. Ballard had calculated the likely undersea currents in the area based on information in the historical record of the *Titanic* sinking and used that calculation to determine where the liner's debris field was likely to be. He began to do his own "lawn mowing" in an east-west direction, hoping to cross the debris field, which he believed would stretch north to south.

This new approach at first worked no better than the old one. Day after day, *Argo*'s videos showed nothing but sandy bottom. Ballard grew more and more discouraged, especially after a frightening accident on the morning of August 28 when the cable linking *Argo* to *Knorr* almost snapped. Fortunately, the team recovered the

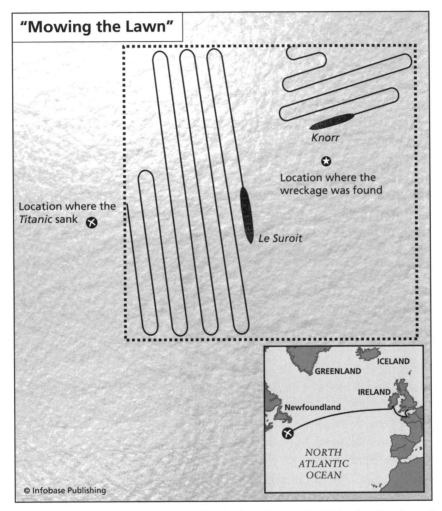

This diagram shows the paths followed by the French research ship Le Suroit as it used sonar to hunt for the wreckage of Titanic between July 5 and August 6, 1985, and by the WHOI vessel Knorr as it continued the search visually with the ROV Argo later in August. Robert Ballard and his French coleader, Jean-Louis Michel, called these regular back-and-forth tracks "mowing the lawn." The cross represents the position of Titanic when it sank, according to contemporary accounts; the star shows where the famous liner's wreckage was actually found.

A Busy Team

During the search for *Titanic*, teams of experts from Robert Ballard's crew manned *Argo*'s control van around the clock. The van, made from two shipping containers joined together, sat on *Knorr*'s rear deck. In *The Discovery of the* Titanic, Ballard wrote that he thought of the van as "the bridge of an imaginary submarine." A desk and a chart table occupied its center, while a row of consoles and television monitors lined one wall. The monitors were his virtual submarine's windows on the sea.

The control-van crew was divided into three teams. Each team worked a four-hour "watch" and then had eight hours to rest. Every day contained six four-hour watch periods, so each crew member worked two watches a day.

Each team had seven members with different jobs. At the front of the bank of consoles sat *Argo*'s "flyer," the person who controlled the winch that raised and lowered the ROV's cable and thereby determined the robot's height above the seafloor. The navigator sat next to the flyer, monitoring signals from the sound transponder network that the expedition had placed around the underwater site for guidance. The navigator knew precisely where both *Argo* and *Knorr* were at all times. On the other side of the navigator, the driver used joysticks like those on video games to control *Knorr*'s movements. The ship had a dynamic positioning system, whose computerized signals to its two propellers helped it maintain its position even in rough seas.

The computers of the *Argo* engineer's workstation were in the van's right-hand corner. The engineer was always alert for mechanical troubles or other problems with the device. Next came the sonar operator, watching the changing heights and depths of the sea bottom and the sonar records of objects found there. A member of the documentation group stood by, ready to photograph and videotape any exciting find made during the watch. The last and perhaps busiest member of the team was the data logger, who moved constantly from one workstation to another to collect data and record it on the map that covered the chart table.

Robert Ballard was not a member of any team; rather, as leader, he took part in all of them. Day or night, he was usually in the control room, sitting at the chart table or moving from workstation to workstation. Victoria Kaharl wrote in *Water Baby* that in Ballard's early days at WHOI, his colleagues wondered if the "White Tornado" ever slept. As the search for *Titanic* went on, his fellow crew members on *Knorr* must have wondered the same thing. As Ballard put it, "My job was to be where the action was, whether at two in the morning or two in the afternoon; sleep would come when I got it."

precious sled and found that the inner part of the cable, which carried the ROV's video feeds, had not been damaged.

"Wreckage!"

Just after midnight on September 1, Ballard went to his cabin for some much-needed rest. The weather forecast had said a storm was on the way, and he wanted to be ready for it. He put on his flannel pajamas and began to read the autobiography of Chuck Yeager, a record-setting test pilot. He hoped that the story of Yeager's successes would take his mind off his own potential failure.

Meanwhile, in the control van on *Knorr*'s deck, Jean-Louis Michel and his late-night watch team—"the Watch of Quiet Excellence," as they called themselves—were on the job. *Argo* was starting to scan a small area near the northeastern border of the territory that *Le Suroit*'s sonar had covered. Bad weather and a strong ocean current had caused the French ship to miss that particular spot.

For the first part of the watch, the team saw only the endless dunes of undersea sediment that had bored them on so many earlier nights. Then, at a little before 1 A.M., Stu Harris, *Argo*'s chief designer, announced suddenly, "There's something." He switched the video monitor's view from *Argo*'s forward camera to its downward-looking one.

"Wreckage!" shouted Bill Lange, a young Woods Hole scientist. With mounting excitement, the other team members agreed that they were seeing debris from a ship. At first, they were not sure that it belonged to *Titanic*, since many vessels had been lost in that busy trans-Atlantic shipping lane during the years. Soon, however, they spotted riveted hull plates, which were used only during the period in which *Titanic* had been built.

The crew knew that someone should wake Ballard, but they could not tear themselves away from the monitors. Finally the ship's new cook wandered into the van, and the group assigned the job to him.

Meanwhile, at 1:05, a circular shape swam into view. Three smaller circles appeared on its metallic surface. "It's a boiler!" Bill Lange cried. *Titanic*'s 29 huge boilers had provided the steam energy that powered the ship.

The more cautious Michel pulled out an article about the *Titanic*'s construction. One of its illustrations showed some of the ship's boilers in the factory where they had been made. Sure enough, the picture matched the object on the screen; the small circles were the boiler's vents. "Yes, eet *ees* a boiler," Michel finally announced.

Meanwhile, the cook told Ballard that the watch wanted him to look at something. Ballard immediately yanked a jumpsuit on over his pajamas and dashed down three decks to the control van. He arrived just in time to hear the word *boiler*. Struck almost dumb with amazement, he could only murmur, "God damn. . . . God damn."

"It was not luck," Michel told him quietly. "We earned it."

Titanic at Last

Lacking the traditional champagne, the crew toasted their success in cups of Mateus, a sparkling pink wine they had bought in the Azores. Then, at about 2:00 A.M., the crew's mood of jubilation suddenly turned somber. They realized that they had rediscovered *Titanic* at almost the same hour that the ship had sunk: Reports from the disaster stated that the liner had disappeared beneath the waves at 2:20 A.M. This thought reminded the group that the *Titanic* site was, essentially, a cemetery.

Ballard asked everyone to gather on *Knorr*'s fantail, a popular shipboard meeting place. There, at exactly 2:20 A.M., Ballard and the navy representative raised the flag of Harland & Wolff, *Titanic*'s builder. At Ballard's request, the group observed several minutes of silence in respect for the dead. Ballard saw that the sky was clear and filled with stars, just as it had been on the night the mighty ship sank.

The next morning, *Knorr*'s surface-mounted echo sounder spotted a "really big target," which Ballard assumed was the main part of the *Titanic*'s hull. He sent *Argo* down for a look, but he knew that the team's "flyer" would have to proceed carefully; if the wreck's masts and rigging were still intact, they could trap or mangle the valuable device.

Argo's video monitors finally revealed the side of the ship's bow, sitting upright on the muddy bottom. Ballard recognized the boat deck, the uppermost deck level. He saw a gaping hole that had once held one of the ship's funnels and then the remains of two large cargo cranes. At last, he identified *Titanic*'s fallen mast. It still sported the crow's nest, the once-high perch from which a lookout had spotted the deadly iceberg on that fatal April night.

During the two and a half days of expedition time remaining to them, Ballard and the others aboard *Knorr* slept hardly at all. They made two more passes over the ship with *Argo*, gathering video pictures of different parts of the wreckage. Only the front half of *Titanic*'s hull was visible.

The predicted storm finally arrived, making the use of *Argo* too risky. The group therefore turned back to the less sensitive but sturdier ANGUS, the reliable "dope on a rope." ANGUS could not produce video, but it took thousands of color photographs of *Titanic* and its debris. The debris field held numerous items that the ship's passengers and crew had once used, including teacups, wine bottles, and a silver serving plate. Later, long after *Knorr* had returned to shore, analysis of some of the ANGUS photos revealed that the stern, or rear, half of *Titanic* was partly buried in sediment about 2,000 feet (610 m) south of the bow.

Media Storm

Knorr began its journey back to Woods Hole on the morning of September 5. Ballard now had to change his focus from exploration to its nerve-racking aftermath: handling the news media. He had made extremely limited and cautious announcements so far, but word of his historic find nonetheless had leaked out. An early story broke in the London *Observer* on the very day the expedition discovered the *Titanic*; Ballard was never sure how the paper had gotten the news so quickly. Tabloids printed various rumors and falsehoods, including reports that Ballard's group was salvaging souvenirs from the wreck. At John Steele's request, Ballard gave several short radio interviews while still on *Knorr* in an attempt to clear up the misunderstandings.

The first reporters to reach the expedition directly were a television crew from the Canadian Broadcasting Company (CBC). Their helicopter flew over *Knorr* on the morning of September 1, just a few hours after *Titanic* had been found. They did not know about the discovery; they were simply checking on the expedition's progress. The Canadians asked permission to land and film an interview, but Ballard had to refuse, even though their network had provided part of his documentation budget. He and the French had agreed that all networks, both U.S. and French, would receive the same material at the same time. Instead, he sent the helicopter away with three copies of a videotape showing *Argo*'s footage of the boiler and a film of the celebration in the van: one for WHOI, one for IFREMER headquarters in Paris, and one to be shared among the world press outlets.

Unfortunately, all this caution proved worthless: CBC sent the images to the CBS network in the United States by satellite, so that network was able to broadcast them before the other networks had received them. Naturally, the rival networks were furious.

That proved to be just the beginning of a storm of bad feelings. Ballard's group wanted to send out some of ANGUS's best color photos of the wreck, but this time they tried to keep better control of them. The photos went back on a second helicopter with both a U.S. and a French representative. The Frenchman was supposed to take his copies of the pictures to Paris via the supersonic jet *Concorde*. The plan was for IFREMER to release them to the media there at the same time the U.S. copies were released at Woods Hole.

That attempt at fairness also failed. Under tremendous pressure from the U.S. media, John Steele released WHOI's set of pictures early. TV networks in the United States therefore showed the images sooner than their French counterparts. IFREMER representatives were so angry that they threatened to sue the institution. Even though the leak was not his fault, Ballard felt that a chilly shadow had been cast over the happy relationship that he had shared with his French colleagues until then.

Anxious to keep matters from becoming any worse, Ballard thought of a clever dodge to prevent the remaining videotapes and still photos from being released. He knew that the navy could classify the data on any sunken ship it investigated as Top Secret if evidence suggested that the ship might contain human remains. Ballard remembered a photograph that ANGUS had taken of several pairs of

Some of the most moving objects that Ballard's expeditions saw in Titanic's debris field were shoes that had once been worn by the ship's unlucky passengers. These shoes were photographed in 2004, but Ballard used similar ones photographed in 1985 as evidence that the wreckage might contain human remains, thus forcing the navy to protect his expedition's photographs from premature release to hungry news media. (NOAA/Institute for Exploration/University of Rhode Island; URL: http://www.noaanews.noaa. gov/stories2004/s2248.htm)

high-topped shoes, lying side by side on the seafloor. It was unlikely that the shoes in each pair would have stayed together unless people had been wearing them when they sank. Although Ballard seriously doubted whether any remains actually still existed in the *Titanic* wreckage, he persuaded the naval officer on *Knorr* to consider the shoes as evidence of possible human remains and classify the rest of the photos.

Ballard knew that his find would attract worldwide attention, but he could not believe the size of the throng that waited on the dock when *Knorr* reached Woods Hole on the morning of September 9. As the precious photos were hustled into a navy van and driven away, Ballard and his crew were welcomed like astronauts returning from the Moon.

During the next several days, the exhausted Ballard gave press conference after press conference. In the main conference at WHOI, he and Jean-Louis Michel praised one another and the spirit of French-U.S. cooperation. Ballard also urged future investigators to respect the people who had died aboard the luxury liner and leave the wreck unsalvaged. "The *Titanic* lies in 13,000 feet [3,962 m] of water on a gently sloping alpine-like countryside overlooking a small canyon below," he said. "It is a quiet and peaceful and fitting place for the remains of this greatest of sea tragedies to rest. May it forever remain that way."

A Closer Look

Ballard returned to *Titanic* in summer 1986 with reinforcements, both old and new. His funding came from familiar sources, the navy and *National Geographic*. His equipment also included two old friends, ANGUS and *Alvin*, the latter of which now rode on a new mother ship, *Atlantis II*. On the other hand, Ballard also brought a brand-new ROV, *Jason Junior* (*JJ* for short), for its first sea tests. *JJ*, which Ballard called a "swimming eyeball," was a smaller and simpler prototype for *Jason*. (Ballard's engineering team planned for *Jason* to have color cameras and manipulator arms, both of which *JJ* lacked.)

In his return expedition to Titanic in 1986, Ballard introduced a new remotely operated vehicle that he called Jason Jr., shown here on the deck of the WHOI research ship Atlantis II. This ROV, a simpler prototype for a planned ROV named Jason, lacked manipulator arms and was mainly a "swimming eyeball," as Ballard put it. He used it to photograph the interior of the wreck, including the spot where the liner's grand staircase had once stood. (AP Images)

JJ would ride in a "garage" on the front of *Alvin* until Ballard was ready to call on it. It would then be released and guided from the submersible by means of a 250-foot (76-m) fiber-optic tether.

At the same time, Ballard lacked an important source of help that he had had on his 1985 cruise: the French. The anger resulting from the media circus after that voyage had been smoothed over, but Ballard's French colleagues had been unable to obtain funding to continue their examination of *Titanic.*

Atlantis II reached the *Titanic* site on July 12. Finding the wreck was easy this time because the team knew exactly where to look: They simply sailed to the latitude and longitude coordinates that they had obtained by satellite the previous year and stored in the ship's computer. That proved to be just about the only part of the cruise that *was* easy, however. A combination of weather and mechanical malfunctions, some in *Alvin* and some in *JJ*, hampered the expedition from its beginning.

When the equipment did work, it more than fufilled Ballard's hopes. *Alvin* explored different parts of the wreck in 11 dives during a period of 12 days. The second of these dives gave Ballard his first in-person look at the goal that he had pursued for so long. "Suddenly, out of the submarine night, a huge black shape loomed up—the knife edge of the great ship's bow plowing the bottom mud into a great wave and coming right at me," he wrote in *The Discovery of the* Titanic.

Ballard found that most of the beautiful wood paneling that once decorated the luxury liner was gone, replaced by clusters of small tubes formerly inhabited by the organisms that had eaten the wood. Only the metal parts of the ship remained, and these were covered with growths of rust that dangled from every protruding piece like stalactites in a cave. Bacteria had fed on the iron in the wreck and changed it to iron oxide, which formed these "rusticles," as Ballard called them. The growths were very fragile, crumbling into clouds of reddish dust if the submersible so much as brushed them.

JJ photographed spots where *Alvin* could not safely go, including many sites on the wreck that had played major parts in *Titanic's* life and death. On its first successful dive, the little ROV "flew" down the area where the ship's grand staircase had once stood, covered with an elaborate glass dome. The staircase itself, made of expensive wood, was long gone, but some of the chandelierlike ceiling fixtures that hung near the impressive structure remained. One was decorated by a feathery sea pen, a marine organism similar to coral, which "turn[ed] it into a crystal crown with a feather on top," as Ballard wrote.

Ballard and his 50-person team went on to explore and photograph the ship's entire forward section, "looking through windows out of which people had once looked, decks along which they had walked, rooms where they had slept, joked, made love," he wrote in *The Discovery of the* Titanic. They also briefly examined the ship's more heavily damaged stern section. *JJ* took 60 hours of video film during the expedition, and faithful ANGUS snapped 75,000 color photographs. Before his time on the wreck ended, Ballard left a plaque on the stern to honor the memory of his friend Bill Tantum and the people who had died on the doomed liner. He placed a second plaque, donated by the Explorers' Club, a New York group, on the bow as well.

The group also photographed *Titanic*'s debris field, which revealed innumerable souvenirs of the ship's crew, its wealthy first- and second-class passengers, and the anything-but-wealthy travelers, mostly immigrants, in third class: teacups (one balanced atop one of the ship's massive boilers, perhaps left there by a crew member), copper cooking pots and pans, bedsprings, space heaters, hair brushes, and the eerily smiling head of a child's porcelain doll. Ballard even spotted a safe on the sea bottom and, though he had promised himself not to salvage any artifacts, he could not resist trying to open it with *Alvin*'s claw. He failed; the handle turned, but the door was rusted shut. He photographed the metal box and then left it behind. Looking at the photos later, he saw that the bottom of the safe had rusted out, so any treasure it might have contained was long gone.

Founding a New Field

Ballard's investigation of the *Titanic* wreck shed interesting new light on historical accounts of the liner's disastrous end. For instance, although he could not be completely sure, his examination strongly suggested that, contrary to common impressions, the iceberg that sank the ship did not tear a gash in its hull. Instead, it buckled the hull plates and forced them apart, allowing the sea to pour in. The location where Ballard found *Titanic* also indicated to him that the liner *Californian* must have been a mere 4 to 10 miles (6 to 16 km) from the damaged ship at the time of the latter's sinking, not more than 19 miles (31 km) away as Stanley Lord, *Californian*'s captain, later claimed. This meant that *Californian* could have arrived at the disaster site much sooner than it did, probably saving many lives.

The significance of Ballard's work, however, reached far beyond this single oceanic disaster. As he noted in *The Discovery of the* Titanic, his 1986 expedition "demonstrated the effectiveness of a visual search in deep water." As a result of his success, he wrote, most future searches for sunken ships would probably combine visual imaging with the more traditional sonar. His video exploration of the *Titanic* with *JJ* was also a pioneering use of new technology: "For the first time, a remotely operated vehicle was crucial to the success of a deep undersea mission." With these techniques, Robert Ballard was establishing the base of a new scientific field, deepwater archaeology.

On July 25, Ballard had to honor *Alvin* and *Atlantis II*'s other commitments and leave *Titanic* once more. He would have liked to explore the ship further, but he knew that he might never see it again. Others, meanwhile, would be bound to follow him to the wreck, whose position was now well known. He hoped, but felt very little assurance, that they would leave it in peace, as he had done.

Hide and Seek

Finding *Titanic*—what the August 11, 1986, issue of *Time* magazine called "the most celebrated feat of underwater exploration"—changed Robert Ballard's life forever. He remained on the WHOI faculty and continued to head its Deep Submergence Laboratory, which worked on improving *Argo* and developing *Jason*. He now realized, however, that he no longer wanted to pursue his original scientific specialty, marine geology. Instead, he planned to concentrate on inventing devices for deep-ocean remote imaging and exploring shipwrecks that lay in deep water.

Teaching Science

In addition to refocusing his interests, Ballard's *Titanic* discovery made him world famous. Besides all the queries from television programs, magazines, and so on, he received thousands of letters from schoolchildren, asking questions about his find and wishing that they could fly undersea robots or dive in *Alvin* with him. Inspired by these letters, he decided to put his fame to use: He would combine it with his interests in technology and underwater exploration to share the excitement of science with children.

The JASON Project: Education through Exploration

Robert Ballard founded the JASON Project in 1989, after receiving thousands of letters from children who had been thrilled by reading about his discovery of *Titanic*. The National Geographic Society currently manages the project, in partnership with the National Oceanic and Atmospheric Administration (NOAA) and the National Aeronautics and Space Administration (NASA). Ballard is the project's chairman.

According to its Web site, the JASON Project "connects young students with great explorers and great events" to inspire them to learn science. Through videos, podcasts, Web casts, live chat sessions, interactive computer simulations, and magazine-style print materials, the project takes students on yearly virtual journeys to join scientific expeditions. They investigate such subjects as monster storms, links between species and ecosystems, comparisons of Earth and Mars, and rain forests.

By 2007, the JASON Project had reached more than 12 million students and teachers. Most of the students were in the fifth through eighth grades. The project reflects Robert Ballard's feelings about the importance of teaching children to love science and the world around them. He wrote in *Popular Science* in May 1995:

> The present and future generations of young minds entering this world are no different from the little boy who grew up in San Diego so many years ago [that is, Ballard himself]. I have great faith in their ability to meet the challenges of the future if we only teach them how to dream. And if they do, I am confident the oceans, the lands beneath, and the life within will play critical roles in their future.

The JASON Project, Ballard hoped, would open the door to those dreams.

The result was what Ballard called the JASON Project, which he began in 1989. In this project, he broadcast live television feeds from his expeditions to children in schools and museums around the world. Students had a chance to see a scientific expedition as it was happening, just as if they were on the ship with Ballard's crew. They could talk with expedition members via two-way satellite. By the early 1990s, a few lucky students were even able to "fly" *Argo* by remote control. Teachers used Ballard's broadcasts as centerpieces for lessons or class projects on physical science, life science, history, and archaeology. Ballard hoped that the JASON Project would convince many of its watchers to study and perhaps even have careers in science and technology when they grew up.

A Fearsome Warship

To obtain funding for the JASON Project and his other plans, Ballard knew he had to go on making spectacular underwater discoveries. *Titanic,* probably the most famous modern shipwreck in the world, seemed an impossible act to follow, but Ballard decided

The German battleship Bismarck, *shown here in 1940, was one of the most impressive and heavily armored warships of its day. Nonetheless, ships of the British navy's Home Fleet sank it during its first voyage into the Atlantic.* (AP Images)

on a second target that might be almost as rewarding: *Bismarck,* a German warship that sank in the Atlantic after a fierce battle with the British navy during World War II. This ship, once the pride of the German navy, was thought to lie about 16,000 feet (4,877 m) below the sea's surface. No one knew exactly where the wreck was or had photographed it since its sinking. Ballard began to think about looking for it in 1987 after meeting Burkard Baron von Müllenheim-Rechberg, a *Bismarck* survivor who had written a book about the ship.

Bismarck had been named for Otto von Bismarck (1815–98), the leader who formed modern Germany in 1871 by uniting a number of small kingdoms. As Germany's first chancellor (prime minister), he made the new country a power with which to be reckoned. He was sometimes called the "Iron Chancellor," both because of his unshakeable will and because of his famous statement that "blood and iron" [that is, soldiers and weapons] were the most important tools for determining foreign policy.

The battleship bearing the Iron Chancellor's name was christened on February 14, 1939, and commissioned into the German navy on August 24, 1940. It measured 823 feet (251 m) long by 118 feet (36 m) wide and had a crew of just more than 2,200 men. *Bismarck* carried eight 15-inch (381 mm) guns, mounted in four huge twin-gun turrets. Each gun could send a 1-ton shell up to 20 miles (32 km). The ship had many smaller guns as well, capable of shooting at aircraft as well as other ships. Its armor plate, which made up almost half its weight, was up to 14 inches (36 cm) thick, strong enough to resist all but the largest enemy shells. It had a double hull, divided below the waterline into 22 watertight compartments. It was one of the largest and most impressive warships of its day and one of the heaviest armored vessels ever constructed.

Germany, under the control of Nazi leader Adolf Hitler (1889–1945), had begun to attack European countries in 1938. By early 1941, it had conquered most of western Europe. Britain had held off the German forces, but the island country's survival depended on its continuing to receive the food, fuel, and military supplies that Canada and the United States sent across the Atlantic. (The United States was not yet officially involved in the war, but that country's government did all it could to support Britain and its allies.) *Bismarck*'s task in the German battle plan was to damage or sever that vital lifeline. German U-boats, or submarines, were already doing heavy damage to merchant shipping in the Atlantic, but Hitler's navy commander, Grand-Admiral Erich Raeder (1876–1960), thought that attacks from the surface would be useful as well.

The Chase Begins

On May 19, 1941, *Bismarck*, accompanied by the heavy cruiser *Prinz Eugen*, left Gotenhafen (now Gdynia), a Baltic Sea port in German-occupied Poland. Its orders were to sneak into the Atlantic by way of the North Sea. In addition to attacking shipping, it was supposed to keep the British navy's Home Fleet occupied, thus limiting the country's ability to defend itself against other naval threats.

The warship's departure was supposed to be secret, but the British soon found out about it. Admiral Sir John Tovey (1885–1971), the commander-in-chief of the Home Fleet, was aboard the fleet's flagship, *King George V,* when he heard on May 21 that *Bismarck* and *Prinz Eugen* had been seen near Norway. He ordered several ships in the area, including the cruisers *Norfolk* and *Suffolk* in the Denmark Strait, which runs between Iceland and Greenland, to watch for the German giants and prepare to block their exit into the Atlantic. Tovey also told the battle cruiser *Hood* and the battleship *Prince of Wales* to head for the Denmark Strait. Stopping the German warships was essential because 11 convoys of supply ships, including one convoy carrying more than 20,000 soldiers, were preparing to cross the Atlantic.

Suffolk was the first British ship to spot *Bismarck*, at 7:22 A.M. on May 23. The cruiser had the most advanced form of radar (*ra*dio *de*tection *a*nd *r*anging) then available, so it could locate any substantial target within 13 miles (21 km) of the ship. (Radar, developed in the 1930s, uses electromagnetic waves to identify the range, speed, altitude, or direction of fixed or moving objects.) *Norfolk* soon joined it. *Bismarck* tried to throw its pursuers off by changing course repeatedly, but—much to the frustration and discouragement of the German task force's commander, Admiral Günther

Lütjens (1889–1941)—*Suffolk* always found it again. Lütjens and *Bismarck*'s captain, Ernst Lindemann (1913–41), knew they could not play hide-and-seek with the British for long. They had not refueled the big ship before leaving Norway, and their oil supply was running low.

A Terrible Loss

Hood and *Prince of Wales*, meanwhile, were steaming to intercept the warships. The crews of the British ships were looking forward to taking on *Bismarck*, but they knew it would be a great challenge. *Prince of Wales* was so new that some of its equipment was still untested. *Hood*, by contrast, was considered an old ship. It was the largest warship in the world and the pride of the British navy, but it had been launched just after World War I. *Bismarck* was faster and better armored than either.

The British fleet ambushed *Bismarck* and *Prinz Eugen* just after dawn on May 24, 1941. *Hood* and *Prince of Wales* led the attack. After only six minutes of exchanging fire, shots from the German warships struck the ammunition supply in *Hood*, causing a tremendous explosion that broke the ship in two and sank it. All but three of the *Hood*'s 1,419-person crew were killed instantly or died shortly afterward. The loss of the famous battle cruiser struck a heavy blow to the country's morale. Ludovic Kennedy, a British seaman and author, wrote in *Pursuit: The Sinking of the Bismarck*, "For most Englishmen the news of the *Hood*'s death was . . . as though Buckingham Palace had been laid flat or the Prime Minister assassinated."

Prince of Wales was also fairly heavily damaged in the battle—but so was *Bismarck*. Among other things, a shell from *Prince of Wales* had let water into some of the German ship's compartments and blocked access to several of its fuel tanks. The damage forced the ship to sail more slowly to conserve fuel, but its guns were undamaged and as dangerous as ever. Commander Lütjens decided to continue across the open sea toward the French port of St. Nazaire, where he hoped to obtain oil and repairs, rather than attempting to return to Norway.

Hot Pursuit

The loss of *Hood* and of its crew made the remaining British ships more eager than ever to return the favor by sinking *Bismarck*. *Norfolk, Suffolk,* and *Prince of Wales* continued to follow the wounded warship, and Admiral Tovey called a number of other ships, including the aging battleship *Rodney,* to join the chase. To slow the *Bismarck* down until these reinforcements could arrive, Tovey ordered the aircraft carrier *Victorious* to send Swordfish torpedo planes to harass the Germans.

Meanwhile, Commander Lütjens decided that *Bismarck* and *Prinz Eugen* should part company. *Bismarck* could distract the British, Lütjens thought, while *Prinz Eugen* sailed off to sink merchant ships on its own. The heavy cruiser therefore slipped away from the warship at about 6 P.M. on May 24. (*Prinz Eugen* returned safely to France on June 1, without having attacked any ships, and did not reenter the Atlantic.)

Just as the British forces were beginning to catch up with *Bismarck* in the early hours of May 25, Commander Lütjens ordered the ship to make an abrupt turn and loop back across its own path. This maneuver allowed it to escape *Suffolk's* radar at last. Admiral Tovey divided his ships to block the paths that *Bismarck* might take, but as Robert Ballard wrote in *The Discovery of the* Bismarck, "As the Sun rose on the morning of May 25, the British were everywhere the *Bismarck* wasn't."

Unfortunately for *Bismarck,* Commander Lütjens failed to realize how lucky his ship had been. He continued sending long radio messages to Germany, and the British ships determined *Bismarck's* direction of movement by tracking these messages. Admiral Tovey's navigator misinterpreted the figures obtained from the tracking, however, and concluded that the ship was heading north, toward Norway, rather than continuing toward France, as it was actually doing. Tovey therefore sent his pursuing ships in the wrong direction.

Early on the morning of May 26, an amphibious plane ("flying boat") called a Catalina, flying from Northern Ireland as part of the Royal Air Force's Coastal Command, finally spotted *Bismarck*—the first time the British had set eyes on the warship for 31 hours. *Bismarck* fired at the Catalina and damaged it, but the plane survived to radio the warship's position and return home. That night, a second British aircraft carrier, *Ark Royal,* launched 15 more Swordfish planes. These planes were old and slow, and none of the previous group had done *Bismarck* any harm. One of this second fleet, however, made a lucky hit that disabled *Bismarck*'s rudder. With its rudder locked, the warship could no longer steer straight.

The Final Battle

Bismarck's last battle began at 8:47 A.M. on May 27. Firing heavy shells through a fierce storm, *King George V* and *Rodney* bombarded the German battleship and severely damaged it. The heavy cruisers *Norfolk* and *Dorsetshire* moved in to fire as well. At 8:59, a shell from *Rodney* knocked out *Bismarck*'s two forward gun turrets, and one from *Norfolk* destroyed its foretop fire-control director, one of two devices that helped the ship spot targets and aim its guns. The other control director was put out of action soon afterward, effectively leaving *Bismarck* blind.

After a half-hour of pounding, *Bismarck* was on fire in several places and almost out of control. Only one of its big gun turrets was still working, and even that fired its last shots at 9:31. The ship was still afloat, however, so Tovey's ships kept shooting. They fired 2,876 shells in all.

It was clear by about 10 A.M. that *Bismarck* was going down. Commander Oels, the ship's executive officer and the highest-ranking officer still able to communicate with the rest of the crew, gave the order to abandon ship. Rather than let the British have the satisfaction of saying that they sank the famous vessel, Oels ordered the men to scuttle it as they left—that is, set off small explosive charges and open valves that would let seawater into the ship quickly, greatly speeding up its sinking. *Bismarck* pointed its nose at the sky and sank, stern first, at 10:39 A.M., ending what Robert Ballard called the fiercest surface sea battle in the Atlantic Ocean during World War II.

By then the oily water was filled with life rafts and bobbing bodies. Many of the thousand or so surviving German soldiers were wounded by gunfire or burned by the fires that had raged aboard the ship in its last minutes. Two of the British craft, the cruiser *Dorsetshire* and the destroyer *Maori*, picked up what survivors they could. Even though these were enemy soldiers, the British wrapped

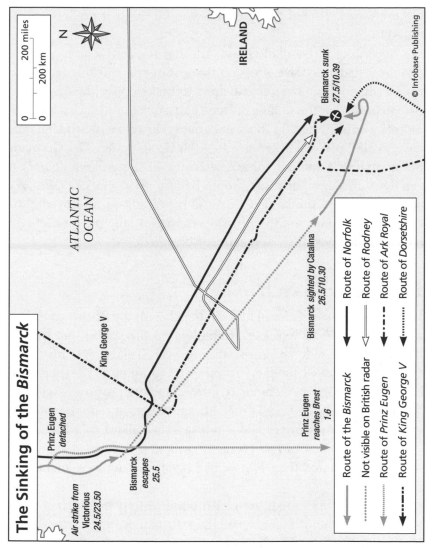

This map shows the positions of the chief ships involved in the battle on May 27, 1941, during which the Bismarck was sunk. Bismarck and Prinz Eugen were German ships; all the other vessels were British.

them in blankets, provided emergency treatment for their wounds, and gave them hot drinks. After only a few more than a hundred survivors had been rescued, however, the ships received orders to leave the area immediately because German submarines had been sighted. The Germans still in the water watched in horror as their last hopes of rescue sailed away, leaving them to float or swim until the icy water claimed them. Of *Bismarck*'s original crew of 2,206, only 115 survived.

According to German Grand-Admiral Raeder, "The loss of the *Bismarck* had a decisive effect on the war at sea." Putting an end to the German warship certainly helped to make up for the damage to British pride that the sinking of *Hood* had caused, and such a boost to morale was important in those dark days. However, the sinking may have made little real difference to Atlantic shipping. The Germans never mounted another surface offensive in the Atlantic, but Dan van der Vat, a naval historian whom Ballard quotes in *The Discovery of the* Bismarck, thinks that this was more due to improved anti-submarine warfare and the British breaking of Enigma, the German navy's secret code, than to the loss of *Bismarck.*

Fruitless Search

Just as *Bismarck* had played hide-and-seek with the British navy during its short life, its wreckage, immobile on the sea bottom though it was, played hide-and-seek with Robert Ballard and his crew. Ballard first looked for the battleship in summer 1988, sponsored by the Quest Group, a company formed for the purpose, as well as *National Geographic* and Turner Broadcasting, who hoped to make a television documentary about the search. Ballard told the media that because *Bismarck* had probably sunk in one piece, it should be much easier to find than *Titanic* had been—but he soon had to eat his words.

Ballard's 1988 expedition had the use of only a relatively small surface ship, the *Starella,* formerly a British fishing craft. Before beginning the hunt for *Bismarck,* the group surveyed part of the Mediterranean, looking for underwater volcanoes and sunken ships that they might explore in detail during JASON Project broadcasts that were planned for the following year. They found suitable sites, but arguments and ill feeling among the crew—including Ballard's own older son, Todd—made the trip what Ballard called in *Explorations* "one of the most bitter and frustrating experiences of my professional career."

Turning to the *Bismarck* search in the chilly Atlantic waters southwest of the British Isles, Ballard used the same "mowing the lawn" technique that had been so successful in locating *Titanic*. He relied primarily on *Argo*'s sonar, though the sled's still camera also took numerous photos to be developed and analyzed later. In the two weeks the group spent on the site, they were able to cover less than a quarter of the 200-square-mile (259-sq-km) area that Ballard had decided, on the basis of somewhat conflicting reports from the navigators of the three British warships that took part in *Bismarck*'s final battle, were most likely to contain the warship's grave. The only debris they found was rigging wire and a teak rudder from what proved to be a late19th-century sailing ship.

Launching New ROVs

Ballard returned to the quest the following summer, but this expedition began with a quite different activity that in some ways excited Ballard even more than the *Bismarck* hunt: the launch of both *Jason* and the JASON Project. This time, he and his crew had a much larger surface ship, *Star Hercules*, which normally carried supplies for oil-drilling platforms in the North Sea. Among other advantages, *Star Hercules* had a dynamic positioning system, in which a computer managed the ship's thrusters to keep it in exactly the same spot even when the weather was rough. This steadiness was a tremendous help when the team was trying to examine a site with *Argo* or *Jason*.

Ballard filled the flat rear deck of *Star Hercules* with shipping-container vans that housed all kinds of equipment, including video and television gear that would allow him to process *Jason*'s transmissions and rebroadcast them via satellite. The crew called the van "city Venice" because, like that Italian city, it had streets that were often awash with water.

Jason was a larger and more elaborate robot than the *Titanic* expedition's *Jason Jr.* In *Explorations,* Ballard described the new ROV as a "gleaming blue cube" about the size of a Volkswagen Beetle, weighing 2,500 pounds (1,134 kg). It had seven computer-controlled thrusters that allowed it to be maneuvered from shipboard "with the precision and delicacy of a hummingbird." It could dive as low as 20,000 feet (6,096 m). It had side-scan and forward sonars, two high-resolution color video cameras, and grappling arms that could lift objects weighing as much as 100 pounds (45 kg).

The goal of that year's JASON Project was to use *Jason* to examine the two Mediterranean sites that Ballard's team had located during their previous survey. One was the Marsili Seamount, an active undersea volcano northwest of the Italian island of Sicily, which contained the first hydrothermal vent ever found in the Mediterranean. The other was the remains of a Roman merchant ship that Ballard had named *Isis,* after an Egyptian goddess who was supposed to protect seafarers. *Isis* lay on Skerki Bank, a group of shoals between

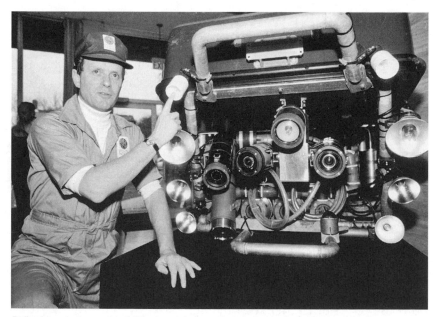

Ballard began to use his full-featured Jason robot during an investigation of a Roman shipwreck in the Mediterranean Sea in 1988, which was also the first of his JASON Project educational broadcasts. Ballard is shown here with Jason at WHOI in that year. (AP Images)

Sicily and Tunisia (on the northern coast of Africa) that had wrecked innumerable vessels.

On April 26, 1989, during a rehearsal for the JASON Project broadcast that was expected to take place a few days later, Ballard was speaking the first words of his script when disaster struck. Just after his team had lowered *Jason* into the sea in a large, heavy "garage" that they called *Hugo* (short for "huge *Argo*"), the ROV's transmissions came to an abrupt end: *Hugo*'s cable had snapped. *Hugo* was unimportant, but retrieving *Jason* was essential.

Desperately, Ballard and his expert mechanics decided to turn an old test sled, something like the now-ancient ANGUS, into a rescue vehicle. Within a day, they rigged the sled with lights, a sonar transponder, control circuitry, sensitive video and color-still cameras, and a grapple on a chain—all the tools they would need, they hoped, to locate and bring up *Jason*. They named the sled *Medea*, after Jason's helpful wife in the Greek legend. The sonar transponders on *Hugo* and *Jason* helped them find the ROVs, and after a tense few hours, they managed to pull both vehicles back on board. *Medea*, however, permanently took the place of the ungainly *Hugo*.

Exploring a Roman Shipwreck

Ballard's crew held their first live broadcast at the Marsili Seamount on May 1. It went to 12 museums in the United States and Canada, where about 250,000 students were gathered to see it. This time, all the equipment functioned perfectly. The *Jason-Medea* team "flew" through the complex terrain of jagged lava outcrops, hydrothermal vents, and smoker chimneys on top of the mountain and showed the shimmering water above an active vent. Through *Jason*'s video eyes, the children watched this unique geology in action.

A week later, the JASON Project's focus changed from geology to history and archaeology as Ballard's group broadcast their exploration of *Isis*. Most of the Roman ship's wreckage consisted of huge jars, or amphorae (singular, *amphora*), made of terra cotta, a type of rough, reddish pottery. The amphorae, the merchant ship's main cargo, probably had once contained wine, olive oil, grain, or fish sauce.

In addition to watching *Jason* at work, students heard lectures from Anna McCann, an underwater archaeologist from Trinity College (part of Cambridge University in England), and Mary-Lou Florian, a second expert from the Royal British Columbia Museum. McCann spoke about Roman trade, and Florian explained how archaeologists preserve artifacts such as those found on *Isis*. As *Jason* flew over the immense jars lying on the seafloor, McCann told the students, "You are seeing what no one has seen for almost two thousand years." Ballard pointed out that the *Isis,* in 2,000 feet (610 m]) of water, was the deepest ancient shipwreck explored up to that time.

Ballard's group systematically surveyed the wreck site, using the electronic equivalent of the grid pattern of stakes that archaeologists would have set up on land or in shallow water. They showed this technique to their student audience during several later broadcasts. During the survey, they found to their surprise that part of the ship's wooden hull had been preserved beneath the seafloor sediment. Using details from the hull and the amphorae, Anna McCann concluded that the ship came from the third or fourth century C.E.

As the distant students watched, Ballard's team used a pair of large tongs on *Jason*'s arms to lift one of the amphorae and carry it to a net attached to the "elevator," a tubular device that Skip Gleason, one of the *Jason* pilots, had invented. Weights held the elevator on the bottom until it was loaded. At a signal from the mother ship, the device dropped the weights and quickly rose to the surface, where team members hauled it aboard *Star Hercules* and relieved it of its cargo. They then attached new weights to it and sent it back for another load.

Ballard's group used the elevator to bring up more than 50 artifacts from *Isis* without harming any of them. The retrieved objects included not only amphorae but also a pottery cup and pitcher, a millstone that the ship's cook had probably used to grind grain into flour for bread, and a clay lamp still stained by the soot from the oil it had burned. The details of the clay lamp let McCann narrow her age estimate to the second half of the fourth century. As Ballard wrote in *Explorations*:

> *Watching Professor McCann teach a lesson in archaeological site dating with that soot-streaked little clay lamp cupped*

in her hands, . . . I was certain that somewhere in the unseen
television classroom we had just ignited intellectual sparks
that would kindle and one day grow into mature archaeolo-
gists and ocean explorers.

Ballard was well pleased with his first attempt to pass the torch
of undersea exploration on to young future scientists.

Hope for Better Luck

The JASON Project part of the expedition ended after making 84 live
broadcasts during a period of two weeks. Many of the crew members
then headed for home, and "Venice" became a ghost town. Ballard
and what was left of his team turned their attention to the still-elu-
sive *Bismarck*, arriving at their Atlantic search site on May 29.

Ballard had only 12 more days of chartered time on *Star Hercules*.
He knew that his reputation as an underwater explorer would be
severely tarnished if he failed again to find the German warship,
making it harder than ever to obtain funding for future projects. He
felt, however, that he would have better luck this time. In addition
to its dynamicing position system, his ship had transponders tied to
the global positioning satellite (GPS) network, which would help the
group determine their location precisely. Ballard also commanded a
more experienced crew than he had had in 1988, including a number of veterans from his Deep Submergence Laboratory at WHOI.
The crew again included Ballard's son Todd, now almost 21 years
old. Todd had been a sullen teenager on the 1988 expedition, but in
1989 he was showing a new maturity and had become an excellent
Argo "flyer."

Ballard planned to use *Argo* rather than *Jason* for the *Bismarck*
search because *Jason*'s fiber-optic cable was not long enough to
allow it to reach *Bismarck*'s predicted depth. By this time, *Argo* had
been upgraded to include side-scan sonar that, if the sled was flying well above the bottom, could survey a strip of seafloor 2,400 ft
(732 m) wide. Ballard intended to rely primarily on *Argo*'s cameras
rather than its sonar, however, because sonar could not distinguish
between humanmade objects and natural ones such as rocks. It

Ballard used Argo *rather than* Jason *to search for and photograph the* Bismarck *wreck because* Jason's *fiber-optic cable was not long enough to allow it to reach* Bismarck's *predicted depth. Here* Argo *is being hauled aboard the* Bismarck *expedition's surface ship,* Star Hercules. (Joseph M. Bailey/National Geographic Image Collection)

therefore would be close to useless among the ridges and gullies of the undersea mountains where Ballard planned to concentrate his search. Sonar also could not reveal small pieces of debris.

The first days of the search, when *Argo*'s videos revealed nothing but the typical vista of ocean-bottom mud, were discouraging. During these quiet times, Ballard worked with writer Tony Chiu, who had joined him on the trip, to outline an adventure novel he was planning to write. The novel would be based on his experiences as an explorer and oceanographer.

By June 4, *Argo* had swept more than 80 percent of the search area without finding anything. Ballard began to wonder whether the *Bismarck* had really been scuttled after all. If the ship had not filled with water completely before it went down, the pressure of the deep sea might have torn it apart, as had happened with *Thresher.* The result would have been many small fragments of debris rather than the single large piece that he had hoped to find. These fragments could easily have sunk beneath the seafloor sediment.

Boots Lead the Way

The area that interested Ballard most lay along the side of a huge, rugged undersea volcano. The team began to find debris there just before midnight on June 5. The objects were clearly made by humans in the 20th century, but they might or might not have come from *Bismarck.* Then, about 1 A.M. on June 6, the group saw disturbed, patchy sediment on the side of the seamount—the sign of an undersea landslide, which could have been triggered when *Bismarck's* hull struck the mountain. Ballard began to make narrow *Argo* sweeps closer together, following the debris track and, later, the track of the landslide. He thought that he would find the hull at the place where the two tracks met.

The most moving sight in the main debris field, which Ballard's group discovered on the afternoon of June 6, was an array of boots, some still arranged pair by pair. Ballard guessed that, like the paired high-button shoes he had seen near *Titanic,* the boots marked a spot where bodies had once lain. A group of sailors from the doomed ship, who had perhaps lashed themselves together as they struggled to stay afloat in the icy ocean, must have gone to the bottom here. When the expedition members thought about these empty boots later, as Ballard wrote in *The Discovery of the* Bismarck, the boots "suddenly began to belong to real people, people we had read about, felt we knew, and who had died on that ship."

Finally, at about 10:00 P.M. on June 6, the *Argo* watch on duty spotted what looked like a wheel with teeth: a giant gear. Almost surely, it came from the housing for one of *Bismarck's* four massive main gun turrets. Ballard and the crew concluded that they had found definite wreckage from the battleship at last.

Ballard was sure that the ship's hull must lie nearby, but the entire next day's search failed to reveal it. By 3:00 A.M. on June 8, Ballard was exhausted and retired to his cabin. Unlike the case in the *Titanic* expedition, though, he had a video monitor with sound in the cabin. He therefore knew as soon as the crew did when, six hours later, a turret with guns still attached—a sure sign of the long-sought hull—began to pass beneath *Argo's* video cameras. "We've got it!" he shouted, dashing to the control van in his stocking feet.

Triumph and Tragedy

For the next six hours, *Argo* surveyed the wreck of *Bismarck* foot by foot. The warship was right side up and remarkably intact, lying on an open curve of the seamount. Its four largest gun turrets were now gaping black holes; Ballard guessed that the ship had rolled over as it sank, and the heavy guns simply fell out of their housings and plummeted straight down. The hull then righted itself.

Most of the battleship's smaller gun turrets, by contrast, were still in place. One antiaircraft gun still pointed skyward, but a sea anemone now grew in its barrel like a flower placed there by a peace demonstrator (as Ballard wrote). The fact that the wreck was in relatively good condition supported the survivors' claims that they had scuttled the ship. Only the last 49 feet (15 m) of the vessel's stern were missing, perhaps sheared off when the hull hit the seamount and started the underwater avalanche.

Unlike *Titanic*, *Bismarck* had kept quite a bit of its wooden deck planking. Perhaps wood-boring organisms were less active in this location than they had been at the *Titanic* site, Ballard speculated. Perhaps, too, more wood had survived on the German ship because most of the wood was teak, which is very hard. Teak had survived on *Titanic* as well, but it made up a far smaller percentage of the total wood on that ship.

Ballard noticed several dark patches on *Bismarck*'s wooden deck. He eventually concluded that these had once been part of giant swastikas, the infamous symbols of Nazi Germany. The swastikas probably had been painted on the deck to identify the ship to German planes while it was in German-controlled waters and then had been covered over after *Bismarck* began to head for the Atlantic so that Allied aircraft would not recognize it. Time and the sea had uncovered traces of them once again.

Ballard's group left the site on June 11. Before they returned to *Star Hercules*'s base in Britain, Ballard wanted to leave a memorial to the sailors who had died on *Bismarck*, as he had done with *Titanic*. A crew member prepared a cross from welded metal and the rope of a fishing line that they had found near the site, but some expedition members objected to the use of this symbol. Dropping a Christian cross on what had been a Nazi ship, they said, was too much like honoring Nazi Germany, a government universally hated for its killing of six million Jews and other wartime atrocities. (Ballard wrote in *Explorations* that he had no intention of glorifying the Nazis; he saw *Bismarck* as a "piece of history" and felt that his attention to it celebrated the British who had destroyed it as much as the Germans who had sailed on it.)

To soothe these feelings, Hagen Stumpf, the one German among the expedition members, suggested replacing the cross with a wreath. This was done, and the team dropped the wreath in the open sea at some distance from the *Bismarck* site. In the brief ceremony that accompanied this action, Derek Latter, the captain of *Star Hercules,* said that the wreath honored both the men from *Bismarck* and those from *Hood.* It marked the futility of war, which uselessly took so many young lives.

Once again, Robert Ballard returned to Woods Hole in triumph. His celebration turned to grief soon afterward, however, when his son Todd and a friend were killed in a car crash. Ballard also realized that he and Marjorie had grown apart, and their marriage was all but over; they divorced a little while later. No amount of success, Ballard learned, could protect him from the touch of tragedy.

Guadalcanal and *Lusitania*

Like the *Bismarck* expedition, Robert Ballard's next undersea quest grew out of World War II. Instead of examining a single ship, however, he planned to look through an entire naval graveyard—a place that had come to be called Iron Bottom Sound because so many ships lay beneath its sparkling water. In *Explorations*, Ballard wrote that the sound holds the densest concentration of sunken warships in the world.

A Pacific Turning Point

Iron Bottom Sound lies next to Guadalcanal, the largest of a group of volcanic islands called the Solomons. The Solomons curve for 900 miles (1,448 km) across the northern rim of the Coral Sea, part of the Pacific Ocean, from northeast New Guinea to the Hebrides. Guadalcanal has an area of 2,000 square miles (5,180 sq km).

In September 1940, Japan signed an agreement that allied it with Germany and Italy, the so-called Axis powers. Japan's leaders were bent on conquest, just as those of Germany were. The country soon captured territories in Southeast Asia and the Pacific that had been controlled by European powers, forming what it called the Greater East Asia Co-Prosperity Sphere.

Japanese planes bombed the U.S. military base at Pearl Harbor, Hawaii, in a surprise attack on the morning of December 7, 1941. The United States declared war against Japan immediately. In the early months of 1942, U.S. forces began to try to take back the Pacific lands that Japan had conquered, working their way toward Japan itself. The fighting at Guadalcanal was part of that effort.

The battle of Guadalcanal was actually a series of battles fought between August 1942 and February 1943. The fighting started over an airstrip. The Japanese had taken control of the eastern Solomons in early May 1942, and in late June of that year, they started to bring in men and materials to build a landing strip on the north coast of Guadalcanal. Ernest J. King (1878–1956), the United States chief of naval operations, had been planning to recapture the Solomons in any case, but the news that the Japanese were preparing a landing place for their planes there made the task even more urgent. If the Japanese completed the strip, they could use it as a base for raids on the vital supply lines that reached across the Pacific from the United States to Australia and New Zealand. Worse still, they might become able to attack New Guinea, a large island just north of Australia, and perhaps even Australia itself. If the Americans seized the strip, on the other hand, it could aid their attempts to recapture or destroy Japanese bases on other islands.

At King's orders, the First Marine Division, numbering 10,000 men, landed on the north part of the island on August 7, 1942. The marines quickly seized the disputed airstrip and (with later reinforcements) managed to hold it in spite of fierce Japanese attacks by land, sea, and air during the next six months. They also finished the strip, which they named Henderson Field. The Japanese finally gave

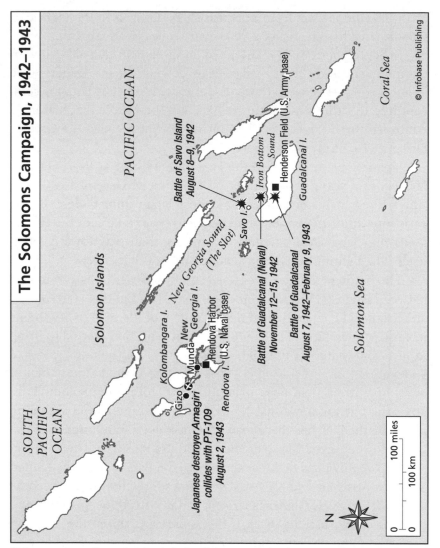

This map shows the main islands in the Solomons chain, the surrounding waters, and some of the World War II battles that occurred there. It includes information related to the fighting at Guadalcanal and Iron Bottom Sound, which Robert Ballard investigated in 1992, and to the sinking of John F. Kennedy's patrol torpedo boat PT-109, for which Ballard searched in 2002.

up the fight and evacuated their troops in January 1943, leaving U.S. forces in control of the island by February 8.

The Battle of Guadalcanal cost the lives of about 1,500 Americans and 24,000 Japanese. It also turned the tide in the war against Japan:

Much painful fighting was still to come, but the Japanese advance through the Pacific was ended. After Guadalcanal, Japanese troops were forced to retreat slowly toward their homeland as the Americans and their allies recaptured island after island.

Guadalcanal's Naval Battles

Much of the fighting over Guadalcanal occurred on land, where American soldiers hidden in the island's hot, mosquito-infested rain forest and on its sandy beaches determinedly resisted Japanese attempts to dislodge them. Important battles also took place in the air. Robert Ballard's concern, however, was with Guadalcanal's naval engagements, especially the two largest ones: the Battle of Savo Island, which occurred on the night of August 8–9, 1942, and the

A U.S. Navy photograph that shows one of many Japanese air attacks on U.S. forces on and around Guadalcanal in late 1942. This particular air strike was a torpedo attack on navy ships that took place on August 8. Despite such attacks, Japan lost far more soldiers and equipment than the United States and eventually had to admit defeat. Robert Ballard's special interest was in the many ships that sank during naval battles near the island. (Official U.S. Navy photograph, now in collections of the U.S. National Archives/Naval Historical Center)

Naval Battle of Guadalcanal, taking place on the nights of November 12 through 15. During these engagements and two other minor ones, at least 41 U.S. and Japanese ships were sent to the floor of Iron Bottom Sound.

The Battle of Savo Island, which occurred just a day after the U.S. troops landed, was a disaster for the United States. U.S. military leaders had unwisely split the navy fleet that protected the marines into two sections, one north and one south of Savo Island, and a fleet of Japanese warships ambushed them at about midnight. The battle lasted only 22 minutes. The Japanese sank four heavy cruisers, three U.S. (*Astoria, Quincy,* and *Vincennes*) and one Australian (*Canberra*), leaving the shore troops essentially without naval protection. In *Explorations,* Ballard called this battle "the most humiliating defeat ever suffered by the U.S. Navy." It left open the water passage between the two sets of islands that make up the Solomons, termed "the Slot," which the Japanese used for a parade of destroyers and transports carrying fresh troops and supplies from their base on the island of Rabaul. U.S. troops nicknamed this steady flow of ships the Tokyo Express.

In contrast to the Savo Island encounter, the Naval Battle of Guadalcanal, a set of confused nighttime encounters that one U.S. admiral later described as a "barroom brawl with the lights shot out," was considered a narrow victory for the United States. The United States and the Japanese lost about equal numbers of ships, but the losses hurt the Japanese more because they had fewer reserves upon which to draw. Among the U.S. ships lost that night were the destroyers *Cushing, Laffey, Barton,* and *Monssen.* The Japanese, for their part, lost the battleships *Hiei* and *Kirishima.*

Exploring Iron Bottom Sound

Robert Ballard decided to explore the wrecks in Iron Bottom Sound both because the U.S. victory at Guadalcanal was so important in the war and because he could not resist the fascination of so many sunken ships in a single place. His old sponsor, the U.S. Navy, agreed to fund his expedition as part of a commemoration of the battle's 50th anniversary. The National Geographic Society, planning another television documentary, also contributed.

Ballard spent a month in 1991 doing a sonar survey of the sound, during which he mapped out the positions of 10 ships. He covered an area of more than 300 square miles (777 sq km), as large as the search areas for *Titanic* and *Bismarck* put together, but most of the

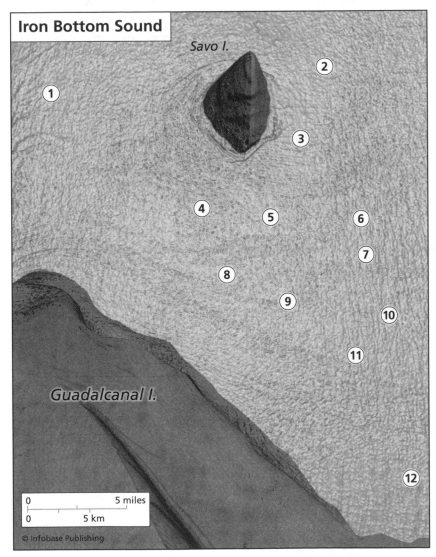

Iron Bottom Sound

Savo I.

Guadalcanal I.

0　　　　　　　5 miles

0　　　5 km

© Infobase Publishing

A map that shows the location of the wrecks that Ballard photographed in Iron Bottom Sound, off Guadalcanal, in 1992. Key: (1) Kirishima; (2) Quincy; (3) Ayanami; (4) De Haven; (5) Yudachi; (6) Laffey; (7) Canberra; (8) Northampton; (9) Cushing; (10) Barton; (11) Monssen; (12) Atlanta.

ships were in shallow water and close together, so finding them was easy. The main challenge would be in identifying the craft, some of which were severely damaged.

Returning in late July 1992, Ballard planned to use the navy submersible *Sea Cliff*, a sister to *Alvin*, and *Scorpio*, an ROV similar to *Jason*, to investigate the wrecks in detail. His surface ship was the *Laney Chouest*, an oil rig tender that he described in *Return to Midway*, a book about a later expedition, as "a large raft with propellers." Ungainly though the craft was, it possessed the dynamic positioning system that had proved so valuable on some of his earlier vessels.

Ballard's small team included veterans of his Deep Submergence Laboratory at WHOI, navy submariners who would pilot *Sea Cliff*, and two historical consultants who would help him identify the wrecks. His new wife, the former Barbara Earle, also joined him on the expedition. Unlike Marjorie, Barbara was a professional woman—the National Geographic Society's television special-projects director—and Ballard saw her as an equal. They had met when the society assigned her to work with him on an earlier television program. They married in January 1991.

During the several weeks that Ballard's Guadalcanal expedition lasted, he and his team photographed 13 ships, including the Australian heavy cruiser *Canberra*; the U.S. heavy cruiser *Quincy*; the U.S. destroyers *Monssen*, *Barton*, and *Laffey* and the Japanese destroyer *Yudachi*; and the Japanese battleship *Kirishima*. *Canberra* had been sunk near the start of the battle for Savo Island, and *Quincy* went down later in the same battle. The other ships had gone to the bottom during the naval battle in November.

The expedition was dogged by an unusual number of equipment failures, but it still managed to take some spectacular photographs. The group found that *Canberra* was in relatively good condition, but the battered *Quincy* had lost its bow. One of the most impressive ships—and, Ballard wrote in *The Lost Ships of Guadalcanal*, also perhaps the saddest—was *Kirishima*, the Japanese equivalent of *Bismarck*. (Indeed, it was even bigger and more heavily armored than the German craft.) To his surprise, Ballard found that unlike the other vessels in Iron Bottom Sound, *Kirishima* lay on the seafloor upside down, with its hull and four huge propellers facing up.

He speculated that this had occurred because either the ship's heavy superstructure or an explosion in its ammunition magazine as it sank had kept it from righting itself on the way to the bottom, as sinking vessels usually do. He wrote that *Kirishima*'s position reminded him of a Samurai warrior hiding his face in shame after a defeat.

As had happened with the wrecks of *Titanic* and *Bismarck,* the ships in Iron Bottom Sound reminded Ballard how quickly and easily human life could be snuffed out. An experience of his own during one of his dives in *Sea Cliff* brought home that message even more forcefully. On August 9, when it was 2,617 feet (798 m) below the surface, the submersible's carbon dioxide "scrubber," which kept the gas in the occupants' exhaled breaths from suffocating them, suddenly stopped working. *Sea Cliff* contained three oxygen masks for just such an emergency, but one of the masks also proved to be defective. As the craft ascended, Ballard and the other two men on the sub had to pass the two working masks back and forth while struggling to repair the third. They reached the surface safely, but the experience confirmed Ballard's growing feeling that he no longer wanted to dive in submersibles.

In addition to Ballard's professional crew, the *Laney Chouest* carried five survivors of the Guadalcanal battle: three from the United States (including one of Japanese ancestry), one from Australia, and one from Japan. For Ballard, the most moving moment of the voyage came as he watched two of these men—Stewart Moredock, who had served on the light cruiser *Atlanta,* and Michiharu Shinya, from the destroyer *Akatsuki.* After they had spoken to each other about their experiences during the war, Ballard saw Moredock place his hand on Shinya's shoulder. "To me, witnessing this heartfelt gesture of reconciliation made up for all the frustrations and danger of the expedition," he wrote in *Explorations.*

An Unlucky Ship

Ballard's next deepwater wreck, *Lusitania,* had features in common with all of his previous ones. Like *Titanic, Lusitania* was a British luxury liner from the early 20th century; indeed, *Titanic* had been built to compete with *Lusitania* and its sister ship, *Mauretania.* Like

Bismarck and the ships of Iron Bottom Sound, *Lusitania* played a part in a war—though only a small one. A torpedo from a German U-boat (submarine) sank the ship on May 7, 1915, when Britain and several other European countries were at war with Germany. At that time, the United States had not yet entered this conflict, which later became known as World War I. *Lusitania*'s sinking did not directly bring the United States into the war in the way that the Japanese attack on Pearl Harbor did for World War II. Nonetheless, anger

Lusitania and *Mauretania:* Ocean Greyhounds

Lusitania, 785 feet (239 m) long, and *Mauretania*, very slightly larger, were certainly built for style. *Lusitania*'s decorations featured white plaster and gold leaf, giving it a look of what one writer called "cool elegance"; *Mauretania*'s salons and staterooms, by contrast, were adorned with expensive oak and mahogany paneling, creating a richer, darker appearance. In 1907, when the two liners went into service, they were probably the most luxurious passenger ships in the world.

Even more than for luxury, however, the ships were designed for speed. Much to the irritation of the British, German luxury liners such as *Kaiser Wilhelm der Grosse* and *Deutschland* had been capturing the coveted Blue Riband, an award given to the ship making the Atlantic "ferry" run between the United States and Europe in the shortest time. The British government and the owners of the Cunard Line assigned rival builders, one in Scotland and one in England, the task of creating vessels that could win back this prize.

The sister ships had to meet essentially the same specifications, but each builder added refinements in the hope they would make each vessel just a little faster than the other. For instance, both *Lusitania* and *Mauretania* depended on steam turbines, a still-experimental technology that they were the first large liners to employ. *Lusitania*, however, had propellers with three blades, while the *Mauretania*'s propellers had four. According to *The Lost Ships of Robert Ballard,* the four-blade design proved to be the better choice.

Both ships lived up to their builders' and owners' hopes. In October 1907, about a month after its maiden voyage, *Lusitania* won the Blue Riband by going from Queenstown, Ireland, to New York City in that the Germans would attack an unarmed ship without warning, causing the deaths of 1,195 people—including 123 from the United States—made many U.S. citizens more sympathetic toward the idea of taking arms against Germany.

Lusitania and its luckier sister, *Mauretania* (which served during the war as a troop transport and hospital ship, survived the conflict, and continued to sail until 1934), were the pride of the Cunard Line, the rival of *Titanic*'s White Star Line. The British government had given

The British liner Lusitania *and its sister ship,* Mauretania, *were built for speed as well as luxury; after winning an international speed prize, the Blue Riband, they became known as "ocean greyhounds."* Lusitania *is shown here arriving in New York City's harbor on September 13, 1907. (Library of Congress)*

four days, 19 hours, and 52 minutes. This was the first time a ship had crossed the Atlantic in less than five days. *Mauretania*, in turn, beat the eastbound part of that record on the homebound leg of its maiden voyage in November. Little wonder that these two friendly-rival ships became known as the "ocean greyhounds."

Cunard a low-interest loan in 1902 to finance the ships' construction. British officials were so generous partly because they believed that the vessels would enhance the country's naval reputation by being faster and more luxurious than other liners. However, the government also planned a second use for the vessels: Along with wood paneling and plush furniture, the two ships were outfitted with gun mounts, cargo compartments that could be converted into ammunition magazines, and other features that would allow them to be armed as so-called auxiliary cruisers in case of war.

The Death of *Lusitania*

Armed conflict between Britain and Germany began in August 1914. As part of its war effort, the British navy stopped ships bringing food or other supplies to the Germans. In response to this sea blockade, which it saw as an attempt to starve the country into submission, the German government ordered its submarines to sink any ship approaching British waters, whether the ship was armed or not. Germany issued an official warning about this policy to other countries in February 1915. The Imperial German Embassy also published an advertisement in the *New York Times* on April 22, stating that "travellers sailing in the war zone on ships of Great Britain or her allies do so at their own risk." The ad appeared on the same page as an announcement of *Lusitania*'s upcoming 202nd Atlantic crossing.

Undaunted by the German threat, *Lusitania* left New York on May 1, 1915. Disaster struck the liner at a little after 2 P.M. on May 7, when the ship was 11.2 miles (18 km) south of Ireland. The German submarine *U-20* fired a torpedo that struck the starboard part of the ship (the side that would be to the right of someone standing on the ship and facing its bow or front). *Lusitania*'s passengers and crew hardly felt the impact of the torpedo, but a second and much larger explosion a few moments later rocked the entire vessel and sent a huge spout of water and debris into the air. The ship began to tilt, or list, to starboard, clearly preparing for a dive to the sea bottom.

Unlike *Titanic, Lusitania* had enough lifeboats and life preservers for its passengers. Most of the ship's crew were inexperienced, however, and had received little training in loading and lowering the boats. The passengers also had not been shown where to go and

Lusitania *sank, as shown here after being hit by a torpedo from a German U-boat (submarine) on May 7, 1915. Outrage concerning the sinking, which cost the lives of 1,195 people (including 123 Americans), pushed the United States closer to declaring war on Germany.* (Snark/Art Resource)

what to do in an emergency. For instance, many did not know how to fasten their life belts, so they put the belts on too loosely or even upside down. Because of this lack of preparation, the foundering ship became a scene of chaos. Terrified passengers milled on the decks, and the crew could do little to help them. Lifeboats tipped over as they were lowered, spilling their occupants into the water, or dropped on the heads of people already in the sea. *Lusitania* sank, bow first, 18 minutes after the torpedo struck it. Because of the confusion aboard, many of its lifeboats were never launched and went down with it.

Some of the people in Kinsale, a fishing village on the Irish shore, witnessed the disaster. They and citizens of Queenstown, a somewhat larger nearby town, launched dozens of boats to gather up corpses and survivors. They managed to save only about a third of the unlucky ship's passengers and crew—764 people out of 1,959.

Lingering Questions

When they heard about *Lusitania*'s sinking, citizens in both Britain and the United States were outraged. Firing without warning on an unarmed passenger ship was unthinkable in the old, "civilized" style of war. "In the history of wars there is no single deed comparable in its inhumanity and its horror," the *New York Times* wrote. Mobs in several British cities staged anti-German riots, vandalizing shops and restaurants with German names. The Germans, for their part, pointed to their warning and to the fact that *Lusitania* had been designed for possible conversion into a warship. As far as they were concerned, the vessel was a legitimate military target.

Although there was no doubt that a German torpedo had hit *Lusitania,* important questions remained about the vessel's sinking. First, government officials and reporters wanted to know why, at the time of the disaster, the ship's captain, William Turner, was breaking every safety rule that the British Admiralty had issued for merchant ships traveling in the war zone. He was sailing close to the coast (where submarines tended to lurk) instead of in the middle of the channel; he was traveling relatively slowly; and he was following a straight course rather than zigzagging, as the Admiralty recommended doing to make ships harder to track. All these things made *Lusitania* an easy target for U-boats.

Mystery also surrounded the second explosion, which damaged the ship far more than the torpedo had. Some people thought a second German torpedo had hit the ship. Others held that a boiler had exploded, although survivors who had worked in the boiler rooms reported no such event. The most interesting theory claimed that *Lusitania* had secretly been carrying explosives from the United States to aid Britain's war effort and that the torpedo had ignited that ammunition, causing the second explosion.

The coroner and a jury in Queenstown held a hearing about the sinking the day after the disaster occurred. The British Board of Trade conducted a more extensive inquiry in London in June. In both hearings, Captain Turner, who had survived, defended his actions. He had been sailing slowly and close to shore, he said, because fog had limited the distance his crew could see. He had not been traveling in a zigzag pattern because he thought that ships were supposed to do this only after U-boats had been spotted.

The judges in the hearings placed no blame on Turner or the Cunard line. The disaster, they said, was strictly the fault of the Germans. Such a verdict was no surprise in wartime, but some people felt that it had not really answered the questions surrounding *Lusitania*'s sinking. A few even speculated that the British government, at the urging of no less than Winston Churchill (1874–1965), then First Lord of the Admiralty and later Prime Minister, had ordered Turner to behave in a way likely to attract U-boats to the ship. The United States had been reluctant to enter the war, and British officials might have hoped that the German sinking of an unarmed vessel with prominent, wealthy people from the United States aboard would make the country more eager to support Britain in its fight against Germany.

Reassessing History

Robert Ballard hoped that examining and photographing the remains of *Lusitania* would solve some of the mysteries surrounding the ship's tragic end. He and his wife made a preliminary visit to the site of the wreckage in summer 1992 and mapped the area with sonar.

Unlike *Titanic* and *Bismarck, Lusitania* was easy to find. Its location was well known, and it lay in shallow water, a mere 295 feet (90 m) below the surface. Several groups of divers had already visited it, beginning in the 1930s. John Light, a U.S. scuba diver, reported in the early 1960s that the metal plates around a gigantic hole in the ship's port side (the side to the left of a person standing on the ship and facing its front) bent outward, suggesting that the explosion that created the hole had occurred inside the ship. This supported the theory that *Lusitania* had been carrying illegal explosives, which had been ignited by the U-boat's torpedo.

Ballard returned in 1993 with a larger group, mostly veterans of his *Titanic* and *Bismarck* expeditions, to make a detailed visual record of the *Lusitania* wreckage in both color video and color still pictures. The team brought several robot vehicles, including *Jason, Medea,* and *Homer* (an ROV much smaller than *Jason,* borrowed from the Harbor Branch Oceanographic Institution), as well as a manned submersible, *Delta.* Their surface ship was a British trawler called *Northern Horizon.*

Ballard found that, like *Titanic, Lusitania* had split in two when it sank. Both sections of the ship were severely damaged. Nets from fishing boats were tangled around the upper parts of the wreckage, presenting a hazard that snared both *Jason* and *Delta* at different times. The ROVs photographed not only the ship but the debris scattered around it, including a woman's shoe and a bathtub with a cagelike shower stall still attached.

Ballard could not find the hole on the ship's port side that John Light had reported in the 1960s. Ballard believed that if *Lusitania* had been carrying contraband explosives, they probably would have been stored in the ship's ammunition magazine. His photographs, however, showed that this part of the ship was undamaged. Furthermore, the German torpedo had struck well back from the magazine, according to survivors' reports, so flames started by the torpedo would have been unlikely to reach the magazine.

In *Exploring the* Lusitania, his book about the expedition, Ballard also cast doubt on the theory that Winston Churchill or the British government had deliberately tried to put the liner in harm's way. "The odds on the ship going straight to the bottom after being hit by a single torpedo were infinitesimal," he wrote. U-boat torpedoes that had been aimed at *Lusitania* most likely would have either misfired or failed to hit the vessel. Even if they had hit, they probably would not have done significant damage—as in fact appeared to have been the case, since most of the destruction came from the mysterious second explosion. Furthermore, Ballard said, bringing the United States into the war in 1915 actually would have hurt Britain because the United States then would have hung onto its military supplies rather than sending them to the British.

Ballard proposed his own theory to explain the second explosion on the ship. *Lusitania* had left New York with huge stores of coal, the fuel for the boilers that powered the ship's steam turbines. By the time the liner reached Ireland, near the end of its journey, most of that coal had been used up, leaving the compartments that had held it filled only with coal dust. These coal bunkers were located below the waterline, and the German torpedo very likely punctured one of them. Coal dust and oxygen from the air form an explosive mixture, and Ballard thought that a spark from the torpedo or the fires that the torpedo caused could have ignited that mixture, producing the second explosion.

6

More Pacific Graveyards

For Robert Ballard, the 1990s were a time of "burning bridges," as he put it in *Explorations*. In addition to marrying Barbara Earle and having two children with her (a son, Ben, and a daughter, Emily), he stopped working for both the navy and Woods Hole during these years. He retired from his position as senior scientist in the department of applied physics and engineering at WHOI in 1997.

In 1995, Ballard founded his own institute, the Institute for Exploration (IFE), to help in funding and developing the JASON Project and his deepwater archaeology expeditions. He is still the institute's president. IFE was part of an expansion of the Mystic Aquarium in Connecticut, and the government of that state funded it. Ballard told a *Los Angeles Times* reporter that he saw the institute as a chance to "meld the worlds of oceanography, history, anthropology, and archaeology" for the public. The aquarium displays

Ballard's activities, sometimes in real time, in its Immersion Theater. IFE also develops deep submergence technologies, with a focus on those that can be used in archaeology.

War in Reverse

Busy as he was with all these changes, Ballard did not mount another major expedition until 1998. Then it might have seemed that he was fighting World War II in reverse: His next target was the water around the tiny island of Midway, where the most important Pacific sea battle *before* Guadalcanal had been fought. The battle of Midway was the first clear U.S. victory in Pacific, breaking the previously undisturbed march of Japanese conquests in the area and turning the tide toward Japan's ultimate defeat. "Because Midway was such a critical battle for both adversaries, and because there was such heavy symbolism in the five big carriers and other ships and aircraft that went down . . . I decided to mount an expedition there," Ballard wrote in *Graveyards of the Pacific.*

Midway is actually two islands, Sand Island and Eastern Island, rising just a few feet above sea level and set in a ring of coral. The islands together measure a total of only two square miles (5 sq km). They lie some 1,300 miles (2,092 km) northwest of Oahu, at the western end of the island chain that begins with the Hawaiian Islands. Today, the islands are managed by the U.S. Fish and Wildlife Service and are primarily wildlife refuges, though Sand Island still has an airstrip.

From the beginning of the war, both the United States and Japan recognized that Midway's location in the center of the Pacific made it vital. The United States had controlled Midway since 1867, and the navy, which regarded the islets as "permanent, unsink-able aircraft carriers," as Ballard put it in *Graveyards of the Pacific,* established an air base there early in the war. The Japanese hoped to capture the base and use it both to defend their country's existing Pacific holdings and to help them launch an invasion of Hawaii or even possibly (or so some people in the United States feared) the western United States.

The U.S. Navy and Air Force had suffered badly in the surprise attack on Pearl Harbor, but in the Battle of the Coral Sea, in early

May 1942, they had shown the Japanese that they could fight back. The U.S. victory in that battle was narrow, though, and the Japanese knew that the United States could muster only a fairly small fleet in the Pacific. Admiral Isoroku Yamamoto (1884–1943), the commander-in-chief of the Japanese navy, decided to try to lure as much of that fleet as possible to a single spot and destroy it in a decisive battle. He chose Midway as that spot.

Plan and Counterplan

Yamamoto planned to stage a fake attack on the westernmost of the Aleutian Islands, a chain that stretched from Alaska to a point northeast of Japan in the northern Pacific, to distract U.S. forces and draw them north of Midway. Meanwhile, the rest of the Japanese fleet would stage an air attack on the Midway base. The Japanese navy assembled a fearsome force to accomplish its aims, including the four aircraft carriers *Kaga, Soryu, Akagi,* and *Hiryu.* According to Yamamoto's plan, planes launched from the carriers would bomb the island, after which 5,000 soldiers, also transported by the carriers, would invade it. Yamamoto, at the head of a reserve force, intended to wait halfway between the Aleutians and Midway. Lacking the U.S. forces' radar, he would depend on submarines to track the U.S. ships and keep him informed of their positions.

Yamamoto's strategy might have succeeded except for the fact that the United States had deciphered the Japanese navy's secret code. Reading several decoded messages, Chester W. Nimitz (1885–1966), commander of the U.S. Pacific fleet, learned that Yamamoto planned to attack an island identified only as "AF." To find out what AF was, U.S. naval intelligence experts thought of a clever trick. They sent all the country's Pacific bases a secret order, telling each to report a different technical problem in an open message. The problem Midway chose was a failure in a plant that converted seawater to freshwater for drinking. When intelligence officers saw a Japanese report that AF was low on water, they knew that AF had to be Midway.

Now that Nimitz understood Japan's plan, he could prepare a surprise of his own. He ordered a small group of ships to sail to the Aleutians, but he divided most of the U.S. fleet into two task forces that would focus on Midway. Rear-Admiral Raymond Spruance

The U.S. aircraft carrier Yorktown is shown here returning to Pearl Harbor after being damaged in the Battle of the Coral Sea (May 4–8, 1942). Naval mechanics and dockworkers at Pearl Harbor worked around the clock to repair it in an amazing three days. The carrier went on to play a key role in the Battle of Midway (June 3–7, 1942), but that battle was its last. (Official U.S. Navy photograph, now in the collections of the U.S. National Archives/Naval Historical Center)

(1886–1969) commanded one force, which consisted of the aircraft carriers *Enterprise* and *Hornet* plus nine destroyers and six cruisers. The other task force, headed by Rear-Admiral Frank Fletcher (1885–1973), centered on the fleet's third carrier, *Yorktown*; it also included two cruisers and five destroyers. (*Yorktown* had been badly damaged in the Battle of the Coral Sea, but naval mechanics and dockworkers at Pearl Harbor had slaved around the clock to make it seaworthy again in an amazingly short time.) The two task forces met on June 2, 1942, at a spot about 250 miles (400 km) northeast of Midway that they called Point Luck. The name was well chosen: Luck played as vital a role as good military choices in the battle that followed.

Carriers on Fire

The Japanese staged their decoy attack on the Aleutians on June 3. To their surprise, only a few U.S. ships responded. Even though he was worried about where the rest of the U.S. fleet might be, Admiral Chuichi Nagumo (1887–1944), head of the Japanese task force, started the air raid on Midway before dawn the next day. Meanwhile, the United States had its first stroke of luck: A Catalina flying boat, the same kind of plane that had ended *Bismarck*'s game of hide and seek in May 1941, spotted three of the Japanese aircraft carriers at 5:30 A.M. on June 4. Fletcher ordered Spruance's task force to head for the carriers and attack them if it could.

The Japanese sent 72 bombers, guarded by 36 speedy Zero fighters, to Midway's air strip. Beating off the U.S. planes sent to intercept them, the bombers did severe damage, but they failed to put the airfield out of action. Admiral Nagumo therefore ordered a second bombing run. The 93 planes remaining on the Japanese aircraft carriers had been loaded with torpedoes and armor-piercing bombs to use against U.S. ships, but Nagumo commanded the pilots to rearm the planes with high-explosive and incendiary (fire) bombs for the land attack instead.

Before that operation could be completed, a reconnaissance plane warned Nagumo that U.S. ships were heading toward him. This new information made the Japanese admiral change tactics once again and order the seagoing types of bombs put back on the planes. When he learned shortly afterward that the ships included aircraft carriers, he had his planes wheeled below decks so that U.S. planes from the carriers could not destroy them. He could not launch an air attack of his own because he had to keep his carriers' flight decks clear to receive the bombers and fighters returning from the first raid on Midway.

The U.S. carriers, meanwhile, began their air strikes. The first wave of planes consisted mostly of low-flying Devastator torpedo bombers. Protecting Zeros and anti-aircraft fire from the Japanese carriers destroyed most of these planes, and their torpedoes did no damage. The crews of the Devastators did not give their lives in vain, however. The lumbering bombers distracted the Zeros and kept the Japanese fighters flying low, as well as using up their fuel and ammunition. As a result, when a surprise second wave of aircraft, consisting of high-altitude Dauntless dive-bombers, appeared above the Japanese carriers, the Zeros were unable to repel them.

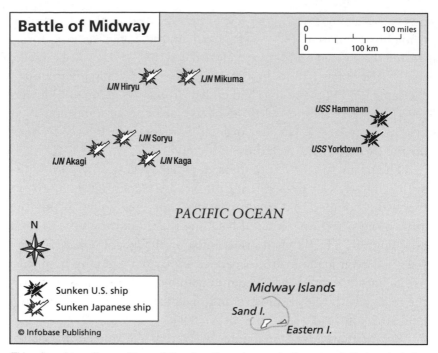

This map shows the positions of the aircraft carriers and other vessels that sank during the Battle of Midway (June 3–7, 1942). This battle was the first clear U.S. victory in the Pacific, breaking the previously undisturbed march of Japanese conquests in the area and turning the tide toward Japan's ultimate defeat.

The dive-bombers streaked down, striking *Akagi* with two bombs and *Kaga* with four. Three more bombs hit *Soryu* shortly afterward. All three carriers immediately became balls of flame. The bombs were so effective partly because of still another piece of luck for U.S. forces. As the sailors and pilots on the Japanese carriers had struggled to follow their commander's rapidly changing orders, they stacked the unwanted high-explosive bombs in the plane hangars rather than stowing them in the well-armored ammunition magazines in the lower part of the ship, as they normally would have done. When U.S. bombs struck the carriers, therefore, they made the Japanese bombs explode, greatly increasing the damage to the ships. Many of the refueled and rearmed planes still on the carriers' decks also exploded. All three carriers became inoperable within minutes. Military historian John Keegan, whom Ballard quotes in *Return to Midway*, called that moment "as great a reversal of strategic fortune as the naval world has ever seen."

The End of *Yorktown*

The most heavily armored Japanese aircraft carrier, *Hiryu,* remained intact—and it was out for revenge. That afternoon, *Hiryu* sent 18 dive-bombers, 10 torpedo bombers, and an escort of Zeros to attack the U.S. carrier *Yorktown.* Only eight of the dive-bombers reached the ship, but they managed to land three bombs on its deck. Two of the torpedo bombers also hit the port side of the carrier with their torpedoes, doing considerable damage. *Yorktown*'s crew was told to abandon the vessel and wait for other members of the U.S. fleet to rescue them.

In spite of this loss, the U.S. Air Force had the last word. At about 5:00 P.M., just as *Hiryu*'s bombers were coming back to the carrier after their raid on *Yorktown,* Dauntless fighter-bombers from *Enterprise* and *Hornet* also arrived and landed four bombs on the Japanese carrier. The ship blazed all night and was finally sent to the

U.S. navy ships sank three Japanese aircraft carriers in just a few minutes on June 4, but a fourth carrier, Hiryu, had its revenge by launching planes that succeeded in crippling Yorktown later the same day. This photograph shows Yorktown about an hour after it was hit. The ship survived until it was hit by additional torpedoes from a Japanese submarine on June 6. It burned through the night and finally sank at dawn on June 7. Robert Ballard discovered the remains of Yorktown on May 19, 1998. (Official U.S. Navy photograph, now in the collections of the U.S. National Archives/Naval Historical Center)

bottom by torpedoes from destroyers in its own fleet. In addition to the four carriers, the Japanese lost 225 planes in the battle, as compared to 150 for the United States, and more than 3,000 men—at least 10 times as many as the United States. Stunned by these losses, Yamamoto ordered what was left of the Japanese forces to withdraw at 2:55 A.M. on June 5. The Japanese navy never again mounted an offensive against the United States.

Yorktown, meanwhile, had somehow managed to remain afloat. On June 5, the navy attached a tugboat to the ailing ship, hoping to tow it back to Pearl Harbor for repairs, and assigned the destroyer *Hammann* to escort it. On June 6, however, a Japanese submarine sent two torpedoes into the battered carrier and a third into *Hammann. Hammann* sank almost immediately, taking most of its crew with it, but *Yorktown* burned through the night before finally going down at dawn on June 7.

Needles and Haystacks

Like the U.S. personnel at Midway, Robert Ballard knew that he would need luck as well as skill to find and photograph *Yorktown, Hammann,* and the four Japanese carriers. The ships were deeper than any he had investigated so far, 17,000 feet (5,182 m) below the surface. Furthermore, as with *Bismarck,* reports of the vessels' locations at the time of sinking differed to some extent because navigators during the battle had had more on their minds than making precise determinations of latitude and longitude. Ballard's team therefore would need to cover a search area of more than 200 square miles (518 sq km).

For this expedition, carried out in May 1998, Ballard was once again aboard the oil rig tender *Laney Chouest.* In addition to his own team, which included some veterans of earlier expeditions but was made up largely of people who had never been to sea with him before, he shared the ship with a film crew from *National Geographic,* a naval-historian expert on the Midway battle, and groups who would manage two pieces of equipment that he had borrowed. One of these teams, from the navy, would control the ATV (Advanced Tethered Vehicle), a 15,000-pound (6,804 kg) unmanned submersible somewhat similar to Ballard's *Jason.* The ATV, which could descend to 20,000 feet (6,096 m), would photograph the wrecks if Ballard could locate them.

The location task, in turn, would depend on the second borrowed device, a side-scan sonar vehicle, or "tow fish," called *MR-1.* The University of Hawaii, which owned the vehicle, supplied a crew to run it. Unfortunately for Ballard, the *MR-1* was designed to fly at high altitudes and find major geographical features of the seafloor such as underwater mountains, not targets as small as the wreckage of a

The Sonar Tradeoff: Range v. Resolution

In using sonar for deep-sea mapping, Robert Ballard always had to seek a balance between two competing values: range and resolution. Since he usually had to map a relatively large area of seafloor in a short time, he wanted the sonar devices that he used in the first, or survey, stage of his expeditions to have a wide range—in other words, to cover a broad strip of oceanic "lawn" with each pass. The way to achieve range was to use low-frequency sonar and tow the sonar device fairly close to the surface, high above the area being surveyed. *MR-1* was a low-frequency sonar device.

Unfortunately, the procedure that yielded a broad range also produced low resolution. Individual sonar targets, even those as large as sunken ocean liners or aircraft carriers, would show as tiny blobs with an unclear shape on maps made with low-frequency sonar. To achieve the high resolution necessary to reveal the exact size and shape of objects on the seafloor, Ballard needed to use high-frequency sonar and drag his "tow fish" fairly close to the bottom. This technique, in turn, sacrificed range: Only a small area could be covered with each pass of the device.

One way around this conflict was to use low-frequency sonar but to drag the sonar device as slowly as possible to increase resolution. Ballard did this in his first search for *Yorktown.* This tactic also had its limits, however. If the tow fish was pulled too slowly, it became unstable and wavered back and forth in the water, which made its pictures useless for spotting relatively small objects such as ships. All Ballard could do was to work out the best compromise between range and resolution that he could and hope that his choice would allow him to find and identify the targets he sought.

ship. At best, the remains of an aircraft carrier would produce a mark on the sonar chart about the size and shape of a small grain of rice. As Bruce Appelgate, the Hawaii team's leader, put it, "You're asking us to look for a needle in a haystack with a vehicle that's designed to look for haystacks."

Four veterans of the Midway battle also joined Ballard's expedition: Bill Surgi, an aircraft mechanic from *Yorktown*; Harry Ferrier, who had flown in one of the few surviving torpedo planes from the Midway air base; and Yuji Akamatsu and Haruo Yoshino, pilots who had served on *Kaga*. As had happened with the veterans who came with Ballard on his Guadalcanal journey, these former enemies found in their old age that, as Ballard put it in *Return to Midway*, "much more now unites than divides them."

Finding *Yorktown*

Robert Ballard had his helpers and equipment for only a month, so he knew that he would have to work quickly. He arrived at the *Yorktown* site on May 2 and began to "mow the lawn" with *MR-1*. By May 5, the sonar fish had covered a 500-square-mile (1,295 sq km) area, more than twice the amount of seafloor Ballard had originally planned to scan.

The sonar maps revealed several targets that Ballard wanted to examine with the ATV. In particular, Karen Sender, one of the University of Hawaii scientists, pointed out a rice-grain-sized spot that she felt sure was *Yorktown*. It was the right size—representing an object about 800 feet (244 m) long—and it met Ballard's chief requirement for identifying a sonar target as humanmade rather than natural: It looked the same from several angles. The data recorded by *MR-1*'s depth sounder also was what would have been expected if the carrier was buried to half its height in the seafloor mud. *Yorktown* had been 90 feet (27.5 m) high, and the depth change shown for the target was 43 feet (13 m).

Unfortunately, the navy's video "eye" developed one technical problem after another, keeping Ballard from inspecting this promising target visually. On May 7, for example, the glass covers protecting the batteries for the ATV's lights imploded, doing serious damage to its cameras and other equipment. The navy team told Ballard that they would need several days—at least—to repair the vehicle.

With his rental time on the sonar device running out, Ballard decided to give up on *Yorktown* for the time being and move on to the site where three of the four sunken Japanese aircraft carriers were supposed to lie. The expedition began its hunt in this area, about 180 miles (290 km) northwest of Midway, on May 9. The expanse the group had to examine this time was a mere 250 square miles (648 sq km) in size. Within two days, they obtained two sonar "hits" that Ballard hoped were *Kaga* and *Akagi*. When the ATV finally photographed the targets, however, both proved to be natural rock formations.

Ballard abandoned the hunt for the Japanese ships on May 12. Before *Laney Chouest* left the area, the two Japanese veterans carried out a ritual based on Shinto, the traditional religion of Japan. They sprinkled the sea with lotus blossoms, water from the country's famous Mount Fuji, and specially blessed sake (rice wine). Haruo Yoshino read a prayer in Japanese, asking for rest for the spirits of those who had died in the battle on both sides. "Veterans from both countries [the United States and Japan] have overcome past animosities and have pledged a renewed peace," he said. At the end of the ceremony, the U.S. veterans as well as the Japanese veterans saluted.

The expedition returned to Midway on May 13, and Ballard said goodbye to the two Japanese veterans, one of the U.S. personnel, and the University of Hawaii group. He then waited several days for the arrival of new lights and pressure spheres for the ATV, which had functioned without them, but not very well.

On May 15, after the navy's photo sled had finally been repaired, Ballard and the remaining members of his crew returned to the sonar target that they hoped was *Yorktown*. He felt discouraged by this time, fearing that this target, too, would turn out to be nothing but rock or that the ATV, which continued to have problems, would never work well enough to tell him what it was. On the morning of May 19, however, the ATV's cameras showed the mud splatters typical of the impact produced when a huge object strikes the seafloor. (Ballard had seen similar "mud balls" near *Titanic*.) It then revealed the impact crater itself and, finally, the unmistakeable outline of an aircraft carrier's flight deck. "Thar she blows!" Ballard shouted. "Bingo! Bingo! Bingo!" They had found *Yorktown* at last.

Ballard's group photographed the wreck extensively on May 20. It proved to be in remarkably good condition, considering how badly the carrier had been damaged before it went down. The team saw the wood-surfaced flight deck, the catwalk above it, some of the anti-aircraft guns, and the holes made by the torpedoes that sank the ship. They even were able to photograph part of a mural that Bill Surgi remembered, which showed all of *Yorktown*'s voyages. They looked for *Hammann* as well and found three of its unexploded depth charges, but they had to leave the site before they could locate the ship itself.

The One That Got Away

In November 2000, Robert Ballard took his Pacific-war-in-reverse back to the beginning: the Japanese surprise attack on the U.S. military base at Pearl Harbor, Hawaii, on December 7, 1941, which brought the United States into World War II. That attack was remembered mainly for the waves of bomber planes that descended on Hickham Field, an airfield where U.S. planes were parked wingtip to wingtip "like sitting ducks," as a famous phrase had it, and on "Battleship Row" in the harbor, which contained most of the U.S. Pacific fleet in equally vulnerable condition. On that "day that will live in infamy," as President Franklin D. Roosevelt (1882–1945) termed it, Japanese bombs sank the battleship *Arizona* (now an underwater memorial) and numerous other ships, causing great loss of life.

The part of the Pearl Harbor story that intrigued Ballard was much less well known. It concerned the portion of the Japanese attack that came through the water in the form of 72-foot (22-m)-long, two-person midget submarines that carried pairs of torpedoes. Larger submarines with the midget subs inside reached Hawaiian waters in the dark hours of December 7 and launched the smaller craft to begin the raid on the U.S. base.

The U.S. destroyer *Ward* spotted the periscope of one midget and shot at it at about 6:45 A.M., sinking it. This was the first shot fired in the Pearl Harbor battle. All five midget subs that were known

President Franklin D. Roosevelt called the Japanese surprise attack on the American military base at Pearl Harbor, Hawaii, on December 7, 1941, a "day that will live in infamy." The attack led the United States to declare war on Japan, thus entering World War II. Most of the damage, such as the fire on the USS West Virginia shown here, re-sulted from air strikes, but the first shot fired in the battle was aimed at one of a fleet of midget submarines that the Japanese also launched. In November 2000, Robert Ballard made an unsuccessful attempt to find the midget submarine that was sunk by that shot, fired from the USS Ward. (Library of Congress)

to have been launched were sunk or run aground before they caused any damage, and all were later found except this particular one, iden-tified as either *16-A* or *20-A*. Because of its importance as the first vessel fired on and sunk in that key battle, Ballard hoped to locate it. "The one that got away, the one that sank beneath the waves, has always hooked me," he wrote in *Graveyards of the Pacific*.

Ballard had just two weeks, beginning on November 7, to make his search. His surface tender for this expedition was the research ship *American Islander,* and his underwater vessels were the camera sled *Argus* (a descendant of *Argo,* named after a legendary Greek monster with a hundred eyes) and its tethered small ROV, *Little Hercules* (*Little Herc* for short). Both had recently been developed at the Institute for Exploration. *Argus* had three pivoting video cameras, floodlights, an electronic still camera, a scanning sonar, and thrusters that would let it hold its position above a site. *Little Herc* sported a broadcast video camera, sophisticated lights, and a detachable manipulator arm. Ballard also brought two one-person minisubmersibles of a type called *Deep Worker*, which could descend 2,000 feet (610 m) below the surface.

As he had done on his other World War II expeditions, Ballard took along several survivors of the action he was investigating. In this case the veterans were Russell Reetz and Will Lehner, from *Ward*, and Kichiji Dewa, who had been a radioman on *I-16*, the large Japanese submarine that was probably the lost midget's mother ship. Ballard's crew also included two military historians, Stephen Ambrose from the United States and Katsuhiro Hara from Japan, as well as the usual *National Geographic* television crew.

Unlike the case with *Titanic* and *Bismarck*, Ballard's challenge during this expedition would be too many possibilities rather than too few. The 1,200-foot (366-m)-deep seafloor at the mouth of Pearl Harbor, where the midget sub was thought to have gone down, was littered with trash that the navy had dumped there during and after the war. The area's rugged natural terrain, a mixture of jagged volcanic rock and coral outcrops, added to the confusion. A map prepared by the Submerged Cultural Resources Unit of the National Park Service listed a hundred sonar targets that might be the midget submarine. Finding out which, if any, was the right one with the limited amount of time and money available would be anything but easy.

Ballard planned to use the wide-range sonar on *Argus* to relocate the Park Service targets with his usual "lawnmowing" technique. He would then photograph them with *Argus*, which had bright lights, and follow up with *Little Herc* to capture details of the most interesting ones. He would deploy the submersibles in the northernmost part of his search area, where steep coral cliffs made use of *Argus* and *Little Herc* too risky.

Most of the sonar targets proved to be rock outcrops, but Ballard's group found several interesting objects. They included a midget submarine captured elsewhere and dumped at the site; two Japanese torpedoes, quite possibly the ones carried by the midget submarine they were seeking; and a seaplane from the 1920s. The team did not locate the submarine they were looking for, however. Ballard wrote in *Graveyards of the Pacific* that he thinks the midget may have retained some power after it sank. If so, it might have tried to return to its mother ship, waiting several miles outside the harbor, which would have taken it outside his search area. Another possibility is that the damaged submarine broke into pieces too small to identify. In any case, this time "the one that got away" remained just that. "But I like the one that got away," Ballard wrote at the end of *Graveyards of the Pacific*. "It keeps me coming back."

PT-109

For his final investigation of a World War II site, Robert Ballard jumped to the other end of the war: an action that took place in August 1943, later than any of the other battles he had investigated (though the war itself continued for two more years after that). This event did not affect the course of the war, but people remembered it because it

John F. Kennedy, later the 35th president of the United States, was a young navy lieutenant when he was made captain of the patrol torpedo boat PT-109. Kennedy and his crew, shown here with their boat in 1943, were supposed to harass Japanese ships as part of the ongoing fighting in the Solomon Islands. Robert Ballard found a torpedo launcher from PT-109 in May 2002. (Collections of the U.S. National Archives/Naval Historical Center)

played a key part in the life of John F. Kennedy (1917–63), who later became the 35th president of the United States. Ballard's expedition, in May 2002, took him back to the Solomon Islands, which he had visited when he explored the ships that sank at Guadalcanal.

At the time of the action, Kennedy had just become a lieutenant in the U.S. Navy. Bored with his desk job in naval intelligence, he asked to be transferred to a patrol torpedo boat (PT boat), a torpedo-carrying boat with a 13-person crew. The small, fast PT boats were supposed to harass and slow down the Japanese ships that sailed down the "Slot," the narrow sea passage between the Solomons, carrying soldiers and supplies to the enemy forces fighting on the islands.

Granting Kennedy's request, navy officials assigned the young lieutenant to active service in the Solomons. Fighting in those islands by this time had moved several hundred miles northwest of Guadalcanal as the Allies dislodged the Japanese from their bases one by one. Kennedy was sent to the PT base at Lumbari Island, where he joined others providing support for a campaign to capture the Japanese air base at Munda, on the island of New Georgia. The commanders at Lumbari put him in charge of a PT boat that had been given the number 109.

Kennedy did not have *PT-109* for long. In the early hours of August 2, 1943, his boat and 14 others were attempting to block a Japanese convoy in Blackett Strait, which separates the island of Kolombangara from New Georgia. Treating the little plywood PT boats as the naval equivalent of annoying mosquitos, the Japanese destroyers plowed right through them. One of the big ships, *Amagiri*, ran into *PT-109* and cut it in half.

Kennedy and his men suddenly found themselves in the water as the stern section of their craft, pulled down by the weight of its engines, sank beneath them and the bow started to float away. Two crew members were killed by the impact, and a third was badly burned by the boat's fuel, which caught fire and rained blazing oil onto the water. Three of the remaining men did not know how to swim—yet swim they must, if they wanted to stay alive.

The 11 survivors held onto what was left of the boat's hull for the rest of the night, but at about midday the next day, they decided that they needed to swim for land. They chose a nearby islet, known as Plum Pudding to U.S. service members, as their destination. Most of the men held onto the wood plank that had been used to mount the boat's 37-mm (1.5-inch) gun as they kicked and paddled toward the island. Kennedy, however, stayed in the water, supporting the burned crewman by holding the man's life jacket strap in his teeth.

The group reached Plum Pudding at around nightfall, after five hours in the sea. They now faced two equally challenging tasks: hiding from the Japanese, who had an outpost on Gizo, five miles (8 km) away, and at the same time somehow informing the Allies—whose nearest base was 40 miles (64 km) distant—that they were alive and needed help. (U.S. observers had seen *PT-109* sink and had searched for survivors, but they failed to spot Kennedy and his men.) That night, tired as he was from the long swim to the island, Kennedy paddled back into Ferguson Passage with a battle lantern and a pistol, hoping to attract the attention of a U.S. patrol. He was unsuccessful, however, and so was a second crewman who made a similar effort on the following night.

Message on a Coconut

Coconuts, which were common on the islands and contained a nutritous "milk," could have provided food and water for the men, but Plum Pudding had very few of them. On August 4, therefore, the crew swam to the next island, Olasana, because it was larger and thus might have more coconuts—even though its size also meant that it was more likely to harbor Japanese soldiers. The day after that, Kennedy and another crew member, Barney Ross, swam to a third island called Naru in the hope of spotting an American vessel from that vantage point. There they encountered two young native men, Biuku and Eroni, who were scouts for the Allies. The two groups badly startled one another. Kennedy and his friend were afraid that the islanders would betray them to the Japanese, and the natives, in turn, caught only a glimpse of the two white men and feared that they were Japanese soldiers.

Biuku and Eroni paddled away quickly in their canoe. Biuku soon became thirsty, however, so he and his companion decided to land on Olasana to look for coconuts. Lennie Thom, the man whom Kennedy had left in charge of the crew members on that island, saw the two and chanced trying to communicate with them. Understanding almost no English, the native men remained nervous until Thom said "white star," the insignia used on American planes.

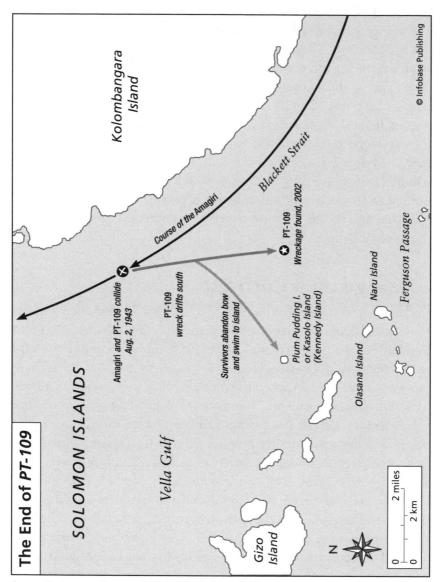

A map that shows the events that followed the sinking of PT-109 after its collision with a Japanese destroyer on August 2, 1943. Kennedy's heroic actions, which saved the lives of most of his crew, earned him a Purple Heart and the Navy and Marine Corps medal for gallantry in action.

Kennedy and Ross soon returned to Olasana and met the natives as well. After asking one of the young men to break open a coconut, Kennedy scrawled a message on the soft inner part of its shell:

> *NAURO ISL*
> *NATIVE KNOWS POSIT*
> *HE CAN PILOT   11 ALIVE NEED*
> *SMALL BOAT*
> *KENNEDY*

Biuku and Eroni took Kennedy's message to other Allied supporters. In the early hours of August 8, a large native canoe finally rescued the PT boat crew and took them back to Lumbari. For his heroism in bringing his men (including the burned man, who survived) to safety, Kennedy was later awarded the Purple Heart and the Navy and Marine Corps medal for gallantry in action. According to Ballard's *PT-109: Collision with History*, Kennedy said that these events, and his wartime service in general, made up the most important experience of his life.

The Real Thing

Because of its importance in the life of a president, Robert Ballard wanted to locate and photograph the remains of the *PT-109* . . . if there were any. The metal parts of the boat, such as its torpedos and torpedo launcher and the 37-mm artillery gun that had been lashed hastily to its bow, probably would still exist. Such relatively small targets would be hard to identify on a sonar readout, however. Survival of the ship's wooden hull, broken into at least two parts as it was known to be, was much less certain. Information about the craft's location at the time of sinking, too, was even vaguer than the location data had been for the other sunken ships Ballard investigated.

Ballard had to obtain permission from the navy and the Kennedy family before he could explore the area of the *PT-109* sinking at all. Once he reassured the family that he did not plan to disturb the site or take anything from it, they accepted his proposal. His surface ship for the expedition was *Grayscout*, an Australian charter boat usually used for deep-sea fishing and diving. His undersea vessels, as at Pearl Harbor, were *Argus* and *Little Hercules,* plus the side-scan sonar sled *Echo.* By this time, *Little Herc* boasted what Ballard, in *PT-109: Collision with Destiny,* called "one of the finest underwater high-definition video cameras in the world." Most of his nine-person expedition crew had been with him on previous voyages. His team also included a naval historian and a veteran who had been the captain of a PT boat in the same group as *PT-109.*

Ballard was able to rent *Grayscout* for only about a week, so he knew he would have to work quickly. He and his team arrived on Gizo Island on May 17. He devoted his first sonar search to a 35-square-mile (91 sq km) area in the Blackett Strait between the islands of Olasana and Kolombangara, where *PT-109* was thought to have sunk in about 1,300 feet (396 m) of water. He thought that he would find at least the stern of the boat there because it probably had gone straight to the bottom. The rough undersea terrain in this area produced about a hundred possible targets, however. He had time to investigate only a few of them visually, and they all proved to be natural rock outcroppings.

Frustrated, Ballard decided to look for the front part of the ship instead. This was more difficult in some ways because contemporary accounts reported that the bow of the *PT-109* had been seen floating toward an area called Ferguson Passage. It might have gone down anywhere in the channel. On the other hand, the sea bottom in this area, unlike the floor of the site the group had just left, was smooth and featureless. Their sonar found only one possible target in the entire expanse. It was the right size and shape to be the PT boat's hull, and it contained several smaller targets that might be torpedo launchers.

When Ballard sent *Argus* and *Little Herc* down to investigate this target, he felt that the luck that had deserted him at Pearl Harbor was returning. Photographs from the ROVs revealed a rusted cylinder of about two feet (0.6 m) across and 13 feet (4 m) long, broken into two pieces. Both the naval historian and the PT veteran identified the object as a torpedo tube, with part of a broken torpedo still inside it. After consulting his reference books, the historian, Dale Ridder, told Ballard, "Everything matches. There were no other PT boats sunk in this area. . . . The torpedo tube matches what we would be expecting to see. The strap matches. The size matches This is it." Navy experts later agreed with him.

The torpedo tube was firmly attached to something buried under a large mound of sand, which Ballard hoped was the boat's bow. He had to obtain further permission from Senator Edward Kennedy before he could try to remove the sand. Kennedy granted the permission, but Ballard's efforts to shift the sand with an improvised arm attached to *Little Herc* did not succeed. In the end, he had to be content with having found the torpedo tube. Even that small discovery, Ballard wrote in *PT-109: Collision with History*, was a genuine piece of U.S. history: "What I had was [only] a barnacle-encrusted torpedo tube, but it was the real thing."

Ancient Seafarers

7

After the *PT-109* expedition, Robert Ballard once again changed the direction of his career. Instead of studying other World War II ships or recent ships of any kind, he decided to focus on ancient wrecks sunk in deep water. Learning about early vessels and the cultures that launched them, he felt, would have more scientific value than studying craft from periods whose history was well known. "I want to turn my exploration sights ever deeper into our past," he wrote at the end of *PT-109: Collision with History*. Ballard also returned to academic life by becoming the director of the Institute of Archaeological Oceanography, part of the University of Rhode Island's graduate school of oceanography, on July 1, 2002. He continued his work with the Institute for Exploration and the JASON Project as well.

Ballard felt that the ROVs and other "telepresence" tools he had developed were suited uniquely to extending the reach of undersea archaeology. In *Ancient Seafarers,* a book about his explorations of ancient shipwrecks, Ballard pointed out that archaeologists previously had been limited to examining vessels that had sunk in no more than 200 feet (61 m) of water, the deepest a scuba diver can go. That left 97 percent of the ocean unexplored. With ROVs like *Jason* and *Little Hercules,* however, scientists could carry out close-up photographic studies and, if desired, retrieve artifacts from far deeper wrecks, up to 2,800 feet (853 m) below the surface. Furthermore, they could perform these tasks while seated in a shipboard laboratory or even on shore.

The Skerki Bank Project

In fact, Ballard had been investigating ancient ships for years, alternating these expeditions with his searches for modern vessels. His first such exploration was part of the Skerki Bank Deep Sea Project, the first comprehensive study of ancient wooden ships in the deep sea. Ballard joined this project in 1988, before he found *Bismarck.* In a series of expeditions that began in that year, he and other members of the project used the U.S. navy's research submarine *NR-1* and the surface ship *Carolyn Chouest* to discover and examine the remains of five Roman merchant ships 70 miles (113 km) off western Sicily. The wrecks were more than 1,500 years old, dating from about 100 B.C.E. to 400 C.E., and lay in water up to 3,000 feet (914 m) deep. They probably sank in storms while traveling between Rome and Carthage on the coast of northern Africa (now part of Tunisia), a busy sea-trade route of the time.

These Roman wrecks represented the largest concentration of ancient ships ever found in the deep sea. Little of the vessels themselves remained, but *Jason* and *Argo* photographed their cargo of huge jars, or amphorae, which now lay on the seafloor. The amphorae had probably once contained wine, olive oil, or fish paste. *Argo* also revealed scattered amphorae that formed trails on the seafloor along likely trade routes. These single jars had probably been thrown

This mosaic, from the third or fourth century C.E., shows a Roman merchant ship much like the ones whose wrecks on Skerki Bank Robert Ballard began to investigate in 1988. The mosaic is located in the ambulatory of the Villa del Casale, Piazza Armerina, Sicily, Italy. (Erich Lessing/Art Resource)

overboard to lighten ships' loads, making the craft less likely to be swamped during storms.

Ballard explored one of the Roman wrecks, which he named *Isis,* during his first series of live broadcasts for the JASON Project in 1989. During a later examination of the wrecks in 1997, Ballard's group used the ROV *Jason* to collect more than 150 artifacts, including amphorae, anchors, and glassware, for scientific study. In that same expedition, they found that the largest Roman ship, about 100 feet (30 m) long, was also the oldest, dating from around 100 B.C.E. Lying in water about 2,400 feet (732 m) deep, it contained 10 different kinds of amphorae from Gaul (now France and Germany), Italy, Greece, and North Africa. A second ship carried granite blocks and columns to be used in buildings as well as sets of clay plates and pots.

Bathtub without a Drain

In 1996, Ballard began a second major deepwater archaeology project, this time in the unique environment of the Black Sea. This almost-landlocked sea is located in eastern Europe, bounded by Ukraine, Russia, Georgia, Turkey, Bulgaria, and Romania. It is about 700 miles (1,127 km) long, 250 miles (402 km) wide, and more than 7,000 feet (2,134 m) deep at its deepest part. The small Sea of Marmara and two narrow straits, the Dardanelles and the Bosporus, connect the Black Sea with the Aegean Sea, which is part of the larger Mediterranean. The Black Sea was part of a popular trade route in ancient times.

Ballard calls the Black Sea "a bathtub without a drain." The sea is a mixture of saltwater from the Aegean and freshwater from the Danube, Dnieper, Dniester, and Don rivers, which flow into it from the surrounding lands. The saltwater sinks beneath the freshwater because saltwater is denser and heavier than fresh. Some of the freshwater drains out of the sea through the Dardanelles, but the saltwater remains trapped in its depths. Oxygen in this deep water is slowly replaced by dissolved hydrogen sulfide gas, the same poisonous substance that forms the base of the food chain for the strange hydrothermal vent animals that Ballard helped to discover in 1977.

In the 1970s, Willard Bascom, a renowned engineer and oceanographer at the Scripps Institution of Oceanography, suggested that the Black Sea might be an especially productive place to look for ancient shipwrecks because the lack of oxygen in its depths would kill the wormlike, wood-eating mollusks called teredos that normally destroy such wrecks. Until Ballard's project began, however, no one

Ballard calls the almost completely landlocked Black Sea, shown here, "a bathtub without a drain." Lack of oxygen and the presence of poisonous hydrogen sulfide gas in the water's depths are fatal to sea organisms that eat wood, so ships that sank there thousands of years ago have been preserved to a remarkable degree. (The SeaWIFS Project, NASA/Goddard Space Flight Center, and ORBIMAGE)

had had the technology to test Bascom's theory. (Western scientists also had not been permitted to explore the sea before the breakup of the Soviet Union in 1991.)

The interdisciplinary team of Ballard's Black Sea Trade Project included archaeologists, other scientists, and students from the

(opposite page) A map that shows the Black Sea and the lands that surround it today. It also pictures the popular trade routes that passed through the sea in ancient times (dotted lines with arrows) and the locations of the expeditions that Robert Ballard's Black Sea Trade Project carried out in the early 2000s.

University of Pennsylvania as well as Ballard's own Institute for Exploration. Intended to last five years, the project involved archaeological studies on both land and sea. The land excavations, which

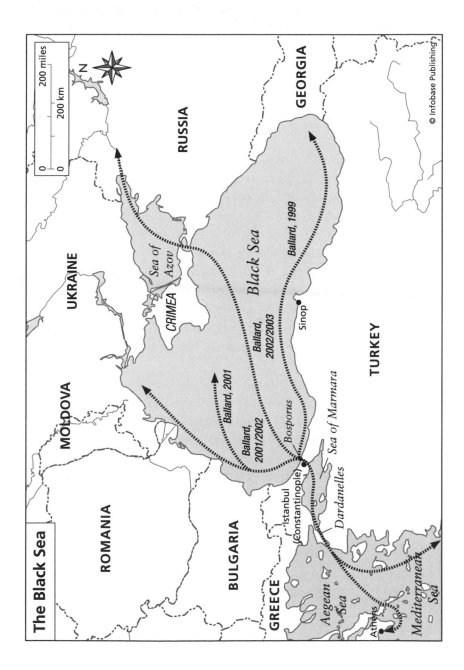

took place in 1996 and 1997, centered on Sinop, once a busy Greek seaport on the northern tip of what is now the coast of Turkey. Ballard planned to conduct the undersea portion of the project, looking for the remains of ships that had sailed from Sinop. Beginning in the shallows near the port, his team would move into deeper and deeper water, hoping to uncover a trail of wrecks that would mark the trade route between Sinop and the Crimean Peninsula, on the opposite shore of the sea.

An Ancient Flood

The aims of Ballard's Black Sea project expanded in 1998 when Walter Pitman and William Ryan, two geologists from Columbia University who had studied the sea for more than 20 years, published a book called *Noah's Flood: The New Scientific Discoveries about the Event that Changed History*. The Columbia geologists claimed that instead of invading the Black Sea slowly over a period of centuries, as scientists had thought, the Mediterranean had poured in relatively suddenly about 7,500 years ago when the ocean waters broke through a natural dam at the north end of the Bosporus Valley. The result was a catastrophic flood that raised the level of the sea by about 550 feet (168 m) and gave rise to the story of Noah's Ark and other ancient tales featuring floods.

In Stone Age times, Pitman and Ryan said, the Black Sea had been a freshwater lake. The shoreline of the lake had retreated during the Pleistocene period (1.8 million to 10,000 years B.C.E.), when ice sheets trapped much of Earth's water, and the lake remained low even after the ice began to melt about 12,500 years B.C.E. because the lake was isolated from the ocean. The lake shrank until its surface was about 500 feet (152 m) below that of the Mediterranean. The Bosporus, a thin isthmus, kept out the saltwater until rising levels in the Sea of Marmara cut a gorge through the land. Floodwaters then "blasted [into the valley and the lake] with a force 200 times that of Niagara Falls," as Pitman and Ryan put it, raising the level of the Black Sea by about six inches (15 cm) a day.

Ryan and Pitman provided several kinds of evidence to support their theory, including core samples from the Black Sea shore that showed saltwater flooding along the Crimea, on the sea's northern coast. Another core sample, from the deepest part of the sea, showed an abrupt change at the 7,500-year mark from light-colored sediment, typical of lakes, to darker sediment containing large amounts of organic matter, which is associated with seawater. Ballard's group thought that if the Columbia scientists' theory was correct, other evidence marking the shore of the former freshwater lake, including artifacts left by the early humans who had lived beside it, should lie beneath the waters of the Black Sea. Ballard decided to look for such evidence when he began his undersea investigation.

The Ballard group's first underwater expedition in the Black Sea, conducted in 1999, found just the evidence they sought. At a depth of 550 feet (168 m) some 20 miles (32 km) east of Sinop, their sonar, tethered to a small Turkish trawler called *Guven*, traced out the curved shape of an ancient shoreline. The pattern of stones, berm (a ledge created by the motion of waves along a beach), and sandbars was typical for a lake shore. The weather was too rough for Ballard to employ his ROVs, so the team used a primitive dredge to bring up rock and soil samples. The samples proved to include round stones that had clearly been worn smooth by the action of waves on a beach. The group also recovered shells from both freshwater and saltwater mollusks, and carbon dating of the shells showed that the freshwater species had been killed about 7,500 years ago, whereas the shells of the saltwater species were younger.

All these discoveries supported Pitman and Ryan's theory that the Black Sea had been reshaped by a catastrophic flood. Archaeologists continue to debate the merits of the theory, however. A number of Russian and Ukrainian scientists, for instance, maintain that no single flood occurred. Instead, they say, water flow through the Bosporus repeatedly changed direction over geologic time.

Preserver of Ships

Ballard returned to the Black Sea for a second investigation in September 2000, two months before his Pearl Harbor trip. He brought *Argus, Little Hercules,* and a sensitive side-scan sonar device called *DSL-120,* which he had borrowed from WHOI. His surface tender for the expedition, as for his earlier trip to *Lusitania*, was the British trawler *Northern Horizon*. His staff included robotics experts from WHOI and IFE, archaeologists from the University of Pennsylvania and the Institute of Nautical Archaeology at Texas A&M University, and students from the Massachusetts Institute of Technology and Columbia University.

On September 9, the group was thrilled to find a collection of wooden poles and blocks of sandstone on the seafloor 319 feet (97 m) below the surface. It "looked like a construction site," Ballard wrote in the May 2001 *National Geographic*. The stone blocks were arranged in a rectangle 24 feet (7.3 m) long by 12 feet (3.7 m) wide. Several of the wood pieces appeared to have been shaped by tools. Ballard thought the materials might be the remains of a Stone Age house, built in the "wattle and daub" (mud over wood supports) construction style of the era. He used *Little Hercules* to collect several small pieces of wood from the site for carbon dating. The wood later proved to be of recent origin, but Ballard still believes that the stones might have been the foundations of an ancient building, set up when the area was still on the shore of the freshwater lake.

Two days later, Ballard's expedition found the wreckage of the first of four ships from what were eventually determined to be the late Roman and Byzantine periods, 410–520 C.E., the time of the heaviest trading between the Sinop peninsula and lands to the west. This ship was about 385 feet (117 m) below the surface. The amphorae in its cargo had the carrot shape and black speckles typical of jars made from volcanic sand and clay in Sinop. The team found a second wreck that same night and a third one on September 19.

Finally, just two days before the expedition ended for the year, Ballard's group located the deepest and best-preserved wreck of all. It sat upright on the bottom, 1,137 feet (347 m) below the surface, with its 35-foot (11-m)-high mast rising proudly straight up—the first intact ancient shipwreck ever found. *Argus* and *Little Hercules* revealed the outline of the ship's entire 39-foot (12-m)-long hull buried in the sediment, complete down to its deck planks, rudder support, and several pieces of wood that (as Ballard wrote in *Mystery of the Ancient Seafarers*) "looked as if they had been carved only yesterday."

The fine preservation of the deepest ship supported Willard Bascom's theory that the poisonous bottom of the Black Sea would prove to be an excellent preserver of lost ships. Ballard was puzzled, nonetheless, because parts of the hulls of the ships found in relatively shallow (300–400 feet [91–122 m] deep) water had also been preserved, and water at that level did contain oxygen. How had that wood been protected from marine life?

Local fishers gave him the answer: The depth of the poisonous part of the water was not always the same. The fishers said that when they lowered their nets to intermediate depths, between 260 and 600 feet (79 and 183 m), they sometimes caught live fish. At other times, however, they brought up only dead ones that reeked of hydrogen sulfide. Russian oceanography texts also described such variation. Currents apparently brought the poisonous, oxygen-free water close to the surface at times, killing creatures that could not swim away to escape, such as the wood-boring mollusks. Most wood therefore was preserved at these depths, even though the water sometimes contained oxygen.

Ballard was busy elsewhere in 2001 and 2002, but the Black Sea Trade Project continued during those years with investigations off the coast of Bulgaria. The project's undersea archaeology team uncovered the wreckage of a 2,400-year-old ship, the oldest yet found in the Black Sea. The ship carried a cargo of exceptionally large amphorae, which still contained traces of their contents— bones from a type of huge (six feet, or two meters, long) freshwater catfish that lived in the area's rivers. Strabo, a Greek geographer who lived at a somewhat later time (about 64 B.C.E. to 24 C.E.), wrote that the Greek army often fed its soldiers salted and dried steaks from this kind of fish. The Bulgarian vessel was probably a supply boat that had caught and preserved the fish and was transporting them to Greece or other Mediterranean destinations when it sank.

In 2003, back on his old friend *Knorr*, Ballard revisited the Black Sea wrecks he had found in 2000. This time he brought a new ROV, *Hercules*, which had been specifically designed for deep-water archaeological excavation. Codeveloped by IFE and Ballard's Institute for Archaeological Oceanography at the University of Rhode Island, *Hercules* included a high-definition camera, a subbottom profiling system, and two sensitive manipulator arms, each with 50 joints and two retractable aluminum "fingers." Another feature of the ROV was a virtual-reality device called a force feedback glove. Worn by *Hercules*'s operator in the control van, the glove let the operator "feel" the texture and resistance of objects that the robot's arms handled. Ballard used *Hercules* to retrieve several artifacts from the oldest ship for archaeologists on shore to date and study.

The Oldest Wrecks

Skerki Bank and the Black Sea were not the only spots where Robert Ballard investigated ancient shipwrecks. In 1997, the year he retired from WHOI, Ballard used the navy's small nuclear submarine, *NR-1*, to examine the eastern Mediterranean off the coast of southern Israel. There he videotaped three wrecks that might have belonged to the Phoenicians, an ancient seafaring people. The wrecks were about 60 miles (97 km) offshore from the ancient city of Ashkelon, in water about 1,300 feet (396 m) deep.

With Harvard archaeologist Lawrence Stager, Ballard returned to the possible Phoenician wrecks in 1999. Again using *Northern Horizon* as his surface ship, he relocated the wrecks with side-scan sonar and investigated them with *Jason.* The ROV took more than 800 digital photos of one of the wrecks and collected sample artifacts, including nine amphorae, for dating and identification. One of the three ships proved to be of recent origin, but Stager concluded that the remaining two did indeed date to Phoenician times, about 770 B.C.E. They were the oldest wrecks ever found in the deep sea.

The first wreck, estimated to have been about 48 feet (15 m) long, was the first Iron Age ship discovered in the deep sea. Ballard named it *Tanit,* after a Phoenician mother goddess who was supposed to protect sailors. The second, at about 59 feet (18 m) long, was the largest preclassical wreck yet discovered. Ballard called it *Elissa,* after a legendary Phoenician princess who was supposed to have founded the north African kingdom of Carthage—the ships' possible destination.

As with the Roman wrecks on Skerki Bank, the wood of the Phoenician ships was mostly gone. The sites were marked primarily by stacks of amphorae, the ships' cargos. (Indeed, in *Mystery of the Ancient Seafarers,* Ballard described the wrecks as being simply "hundreds of large storage jars deposited roughly in the shape of ships.") The larger ship, for instance, had been hauling about 400 jars of wine. The sites also contained a number of other artifacts,

Phoenicians: The Purple People

The Phoenician civilization flourished from roughly 1500 to 300 B.C.E., reaching the height of its power between about 1200 and 800 B.C.E. At that time, its merchant ships traveled all around the Mediterranean—and beyond. According to some accounts, Phoenicians regularly went to Britain to buy tin, a metal they needed to make bronze (a widely used mixture of tin and copper). A Phoenician expedition is said to have sailed clear around Africa in about 600 B.C.E.

The Phoenicians lived in several independent city-states on the coasts of what are now Lebanon, Syria, and Israel. Like most others in the Middle East, they belonged to the Semitic group of peoples. They called themselves *Kena'ani,* or Canaanites. They were the ancestors of today's Lebanese.

The Phoenicians' land was not good for growing crops, so they turned to the sea instead, establishing their fortune as shipbuilders, sailors, and traders. Most early seafarers hugged the coasts for safety, but Robert Ballard believes that the Phoenicians risked sailing straight across the Mediterranean to shorten their travel time to distant locations such as Egypt or Carthage.

Phoenician comes from a Greek word meaning "purple." The Greeks, one of the Phoenicians' regular trading partners, gave them this name because of their most valuable ware: a beautiful reddish-purple dye made from a type of sea snail called *Murex.* Only the wealthy could afford cloth stained with this color, which was called Tyrian purple after the Phoenician city of Tyre. Eventually, only royalty was allowed to wear it.

The Phoenicians also exported other products, including glass, cedarwood, and cloth. They exported culture as well. To help them record their trading transactions, they developed a 22-letter alphabet, much simpler than the 550-character cuneiform alphabet used by some earlier Middle Eastern civilizations. They taught this alphabet to people in the lands they visited. The Phoenician alphabet is the ancestor of the alphabets used in Western societies today.

In 1997, Ballard discovered the wrecks of two Phoenician ships, later dated at about 770 B.C.E., in Mediterranean waters near Israel—the oldest wrecks ever found in the deep sea. In their heyday, the ships probably looked much like this one, from a relief at the end of a stone coffin (sarcophagus). (Erich Lessing/Art Resource)

however, including dishes for food preparation, an incense stand for offerings to the weather gods, and a wine decanter. *Jason* brought up several of these objects for archaeologists to study.

Ballard tried to return to the ships in 2003 with *Hercules* and *Argus,* but the Egyptian government denied him permission to enter the area because of political concerns. He revisited the Roman wrecks in Skerki Bank instead and photographed them in more detail than had been possible before. (As Peter de Jonge commented in "Being Bob Ballard," a profile of Ballard that appeared in the May 2004 *National Geographic,* "Ballard is constantly generating options, which is his way of ensuring that no setback will cost him too much.")

During the Skerki Bank and Black Sea expeditions in 2003, Ballard connected scientists at several universities to his shipboard site by a high-bandwidth satellite and Internet2, an advanced computer communication network established by a consortium of educational, industry, and government institutions. This communication arrangement allowed the researchers to join the expedition without having to leave their laboratories. Ballard expects such technology to be common in expeditions of the future. Such expeditions will primarily use ROVs such as *Hercules,* which has already, as he wrote in *Mystery of the Ancient Seafarers,* "proved that wrecks could be scientifically and systematically excavated with minimum effort and maximum efficiency." He himself plans to continue leading missions to the Mediterranean and the Black Sea. "I know much more is down there," he concluded. "I'm going back—a lot."

Conclusion:

Undersea Museums

In 2004, Robert Ballard revisited the site of his greatest triumph and the shipwreck that is probably closest to his heart: RMS *Titanic.* His purpose was to rephotograph the wreck and to match these new photos with the ones he had taken in 1985 and 1986. The comparison would show how much damage nature and human invasion had done to the ship in the 18 years since Ballard's team had discovered it.

Open Season

Ballard suspected that the damage might be considerable. Despite his hope that *Titanic* would be left in peace, salvage teams in submersibles had visited the wreck seven times and removed a total of about 6,000 artifacts. The U.S. Congress had passed the RMS

Titanic Maritime Memorial Act, a law calling for the wreck to be made a protected international memorial, in 1986, but the law had little effect because the wreck lay in waters claimed by Canada. As a result, "the ship seemingly has worn an 'open season' sign," Ballard wrote in *Return to* Titanic, his book about the 2004 visit.

In August 1987, a consortium of U.S. investors and IFREMER sent an expedition, which included the French submersible *Nautile*, to salvage artifacts from the wreck. They took away about 1,800 objects. This group and others formed a company called RMS Titanic, Inc., in the early 1990s. On June 7, 1994, the U.S. District Court for the Eastern District of Virginia ruled that company to be the owner of the wreck and its "salvor in possession" because it was the first to bring up items from the site. (Ironically, international law denied Ballard's group this title precisely because they chose *not* to bring back any artifacts from the ship.) A 2006 decision by the U.S. Fourth Circuit Court of Appeals confirmed the company's rights to the wreck and ownership of all artifacts removed from it—a trove worth $16.5 million, according to one estimate.

RMS Titanic, Inc., conducted further salvage expeditions in 1993, 1994, 1996, 1998, 2000, and 2004 and retrieved additional artifacts, including newspapers, paper money, letters, and a readable copy of the *Home and School Standard Dictionary* with bookmarks still in place. It even brought up a 20-by-24-foot (6-by-7.3-m) section of the ship's hull in 1998 by attaching bags of diesel fuel to it, a method similar to that used to keep bathyscaphes afloat. The company mounted most of its salvaged objects in traveling exhibits that, according to the company's Web site, have been seen by more than 15 million people worldwide. RMS Titanic, Inc., a wholly owned subsidiary of a larger business called Premier Exhibitions, claims that its displays are "presented in an enlightening and dignified manner . . . that embodies respect for those who lost their lives and that embraces the advances in marine science generated by the Company's recovery expeditions."

Return to *Titanic*

Ballard returned to *Titanic* on *Ronald H. Brown*, a National Oceanic and Atmospheric Administration (NOAA) research ship, with *Argus* and *Hercules* on board. In addition to its own crew of 26, *Ron Brown*, as the vessel was usually called, carried Ballard's team of 32 scientists, engineers, and technicians, including specialists in navigation, video technology, and communication—what Ballard, in *Return to* Titanic, called "the best in the deep-submergence community." His expedition would be linked to distant sites by satellite and Internet2 technology. Ballard planned for it to include live JASON Project and Immersion Project broadcasts as well as a *National Geographic* television special. (The Immersion Project is an educational effort similar to the JASON Project, sponsored by the Institute for Exploration.)

Ron Brown reached the *Titanic* site on May 30, 2004, and examined the wreck for 11 days. *Hercules* first spotted part of the ship, the rear of the bow section, at just before midnight on the first day. "I felt almost as if I were seeing *Titanic* for the first time," Ballard wrote in *Return to* Titanic:

> *The last time here, I had glimpsed the ship through* Alvin's *softball-sized windows with limited lighting. Now I saw* Titanic *as if in full sun, through a bay window. There was no comparison. Everything appeared with crystal clarity: hull plates, bow railings, bitts, and those haunting portholes.*

The deterioration of the wreck, revealed in the more than 2,200 digital images captured by *Hercules,* was almost as great as Ballard had feared. "Damaged and picked over, *Titanic* is less of a ship now than two decades ago," he wrote. The crow's nest, which the photographs from the mid-1980s had shown so clearly, was now ruined, perhaps because someone tried to extract the ship's telephone from it. Some of the letters that once spelled out the ship's name on the hull had been removed. The mast was almost completely destroyed, its remains "plundered, stripped, and sad." The beautiful brass light that had adorned it was gone. Similarly, the brass telemotor that formerly held the ship's wooden steering wheel was broken and twisted, "leaning to port like a drunken sailor."

The deck of the ship's bow section was scarred with tracks left by landing submersibles. Fond as he had once been of these small craft, Ballard saw them as "large and clumsy" compared with his ROVs. They had to land on the wreck to study it, and most of the landings

Ballard returned to the wreck of Titanic in 2004 with a new ROV called Hercules, shown here examining boxes on the stern of the wrecked ship. Ballard wanted to rephotograph the wreck to find out how much damage salvagers had done to it in the 18 years since he had discovered it. (IFE/UR/NOAA; URL: http://www.noaanews. noaa.gov/stories2005/s2370.htm)

damaged the ship's remaining surfaces. Accidental collisions with parts of the sunken vessel smashed holes in walls and twisted metal.

New "rusticles" formed by iron-eating bacteria were everywhere. According to *Return to* Titanic, Canadian scientists estimated that the bacteria sucked several hundred pounds of iron from the ship each day. Some researchers suspected that the human invasions had increased the bacteria's rate of growth by making new cracks and fissures, thereby exposing more bare metal to the microbes. NOAA claims that because of the combination of iron-eating bacteria and damage from salvagers, the hull and structure of *Titanic* may collapse completely within the next 50 years.

Ballard's team looked at *Titanic*'s debris field on June 4. Parts of it had been well picked over, but large areas had never been explored. *Hercules* spotted new objects that spoke strongly of the ship's lost human occupants, including shoes, souvenir dishes, a boot and a rain slicker, a hand mirror, and a woman's hair comb. Just as they had done in 1985 and 1986, the group photographed these artifacts but left them where they were.

In *Return to* Titanic, Ballard explained why he was willing to remove artifacts that he found in ancient ships, such as the clay lamp he brought up from *Isis* in 1989, yet felt so strongly that objects from recent wrecks such as *Titanic* should be left alone. The ancient artifacts, he said, had scientific value; examining them in detail could help archaeologists date the wrecks and learn about the cultures to whom the ships had belonged. This was not true of *Titanic*, however: "We [already] know exactly how the ship was built and what was on board." He expanded on this idea in *The Discovery of the* Titanic:

> *A teacup brought to the surface and restored to "mint condition," with its red White Star Line insignia gleaming as good as new, is still little more than a teacup. However, a teacup resting on a boiler at the bottom of the ocean, as if set there moments ago, is a moving reminder of the* Titanic's *fate.*

Ballard said that he, for one, would prefer the teacup to stay where it was.

A Poster Case for Preservation

The destruction that Ballard saw on his 2004 visit to *Titanic* greatly saddened him, but he felt that one useful thing could grow out of it: The *Titanic* could serve as an example of how *not* to treat historic shipwrecks. Ballard said in a National Public Radio broadcast about his 2004 expedition:

> *By documenting what has happened to* Titanic, *my science team hoped ... to begin to formulate a strategy to counter its deterioration. The knowledge gained through the study of* Titanic *will guide future archaeologists, and the protection afforded this shipwreck could be a model for others.*

Perhaps even more important, Ballard hoped that publicizing the damage done to the famous ship could influence the battle between what he called in *Return to* Titanic "the 'Rest in Peace' and the 'Wrest a Piece' contingents." He wrote in *Return to* Titanic:

> *The future of undersea exploration is being decided, now. How should the more than a million shipwrecks in the Atlantic,*

Ballard, shown here in the control van aboard the research ship Ronald H. Brown *during his 2004 return to* Titanic, *hoped that the damage done to the famous wreck would convince people to ban salvage on such wrecks and instead preserve them as underwater museums.* (Bert Fox, © National Geographic Society)

> *Pacific, Mediterranean and other international bodies of water be governed? Who decides whether they will be salvaged or explored peacefully in situ [where they lie]? Pillaged or protected?... Most voters and legislators yawn at such questions, but they sit up and pay attention when they see* Titanic.

Ballard thought that seeing the damage with their own eyes, through *Hercules*'s striking photographs, might persuade the public to demand, and legislators to pass, laws protecting undersea wrecks.

A Virtual Museum

In interview after interview, Robert Ballard has emphasized his view of the deep sea as a gigantic museum, "holding more history than all the museums of the world combined." He saw the photographs, books, and television programs spawned by his expeditions as the first step in opening that museum to the public. For example, he wrote the following in *The Lost Ships of Guadalcanal*:

> There is no substitute for seeing the literal evidence of war—shell holes in blasted metal, guns and torpedo tubes still trained as if to fire or pointing crazily askew, the wrecked bridge where a captain or an admiral breathed his last. The search for this reality was our real purpose in coming to Guadalcanal—to bring back images that would fill out the story in the history books, to mark and memorialize this great submarine battlefield, to make dead ships live again.

Still, Ballard has said, such efforts are "only the beginning" of what he would like to see. In *Return to* Titanic and an article in the July 2005 *Popular Science,* Ballard pictured *Titanic* as the first of what he hoped would be many underwater museum exhibits that people could visit from their living rooms via telepresence. Several ROVs would be installed at the site and programmed to follow fixed routes around it. Powerful underwater lights would illuminate key parts of the site as the ROVs passed. The ROVs' high-definition video cameras, powered by a moored buoy, would send their feeds back to the buoy through fiber-optic cables. The buoy, in turn, would transmit the feeds as radio signals to a communication satellite that hovered overhead. The satellite would send the video footage to a land station that would transmit it around the world, in real time, via Internet2.

At first, the streaming video from the underwater museum would have to be viewed at sites equipped for Internet2 reception, such as the IFE's Immersion Theater at Mystic Aquarium. After this second-generation Internet becomes more widely available, however, people would be able to make virtual visits to *Titanic* from their own homes. They could even modify the routes and camera angles of the ROVs to some extent to focus on the parts of the ship that interest them most. If such virtual visits to undersea wrecks become common, Robert Ballard will have achieved his greatest dream: to preserve the wrecks and, at the same time, let everyone experience the thrill of undersea exploration and discovery that has so enriched his own life.

CHRONOLOGY

April 14, 1912   RMS *Titanic* hits iceberg and sinks in north Atlantic, costing 1,522 lives.

May 7, 1915   Torpedo from German U-boat sinks British luxury liner *Lusitania,* killing 1,195 people.

May 27, 1941   British warships sink German battleship *Bismarck* in north Atlantic.

December 7, 1941   Japan stages surprise attack on U.S. military base at Pearl Harbor, Hawaii; in response, United States declares war on Japan, thereby entering World War II.

June 3–7, 1942   Battle of Midway is fought, resulting in a decisive U.S. victory.

June 30, 1942   Robert Duane Ballard is born in Wichita, Kansas.

1942–1943   United States and Japanese forces fight on and around Guadalcanal between August 1942 and February 1943, including large naval engagements on August 8–9 (Battle of Savo Island) and November 12–15 (Naval Battle of Guadalcanal).

1943   Ballard family moves to San Diego, California.

August 2, 1943   Japanese destroyer sinks John F. Kennedy's PT boat, *PT-109*; Kennedy's heroic actions during the next several days help to save the lives of most of the boat's crew members.

1959
Ballard takes summer program at Scripps Institution of Oceanography and decides to become a marine scientist.

1960
Harry Hess proposes theory of seafloor spreading to explain how Earth's crust is created and destroyed.

1964
Submersible *Alvin* goes into service at Woods Hole Oceanographic Institution (WHOI).

1965
Ballard earns a bachelor's degree in physical sciences from University of California, Santa Barbara; he becomes a lieutenant in the army intelligence service.

mid-1960s
Plate tectonics theory is established and becomes accepted by many, but not all, earth scientists.

1965–1966
Ballard studies undersea geology at University of Hawaii, Honolulu; works as dolphin trainer for Sea Life Park; transfers from army to navy.

1966–1967
Ballard works on submersible project for North American Aviation; attends graduate school at University of Southern California; marries Marjorie Hargas.

1967
Ballard is called to active duty by the navy and assigned to the Office of Naval Research (ONR); moves to Massachusetts and begins work as ONR liaison to WHOI.

1969
ONR says that navy funding for dives in *Alvin* will soon be discontinued and tells

Ballard that his navy job is also about to end; Ballard makes first undersea trip, in mesoscaphe *Ben Franklin.*

1970

Ballard's navy commission ends; he becomes a research associate in engineering at WHOI; enrolls in Ph.D. program in marine geology at the University of Rhode Island; begins Ph.D. project on plate tectonics.

1971

Ballard dives repeatedly in *Alvin* as part of his Ph.D. research; hears about French proposal for joint expedition to explore Mid-Atlantic Ridge.

1972

Ballard defends submersibles in speech to eminent earth scientists; completes Ph.D. research.

1973

Project FAMOUS begins to explore Mid-Atlantic Ridge; Ballard takes part in expedition and develops camera sled ANGUS; begins to seek funding to look for wreck of *Titanic.*

June 5, 1974

Ballard obtains Ph.D. in marine geology from University of Rhode Island.

July–August 1974

Ballard dives on Mid-Atlantic Ridge in *Alvin* as part of Project FAMOUS; is promoted to assistant scientist at WHOI.

1976

Ballard is promoted to associate scientist; leads expedition to the Cayman Trough, his first time as lead scientist.

February–March 1977

Ballard and other scientists discover unique life forms around hydrothermal vents in the deep sea.

1977	Cayman Trough expedition continues with bathyscaphe dives; Big Events offers to sponsor *Titanic* expedition, but Ballard refuses.
1978	Ballard and French team on Project RITA discover undersea lakes and towers of hardened lava on East Pacific Rise.
1979	Ballard and others return to Galápagos Rift to study hydrothermal vent animals in more detail; Ballard and French scientists discover "black smoker" undersea vents near Baja California.
1980	Ballard is awarded tenure at WHOI; takes sabbatical year at Stanford University (California); begins to focus on remotely operated vehicles (ROVs) rather than submersibles and designs *Argo-Jason* system.
1981	Ballard founds the Deep Submergence Laboratory at WHOI.
1982	Ballard persuades the navy to fund development of his *Argo-Jason* system.
1984	Ballard tests *Argo* on wreck of submarine *Thresher* and discovers that debris from deepwater wrecks forms a linear trail rather than a circle around the wreck; persuades French scientific group to cosponsor a search for *Titanic*.
July 5, 1985	French team begins sonar search for *Titanic*.
August 24, 1985	Ballard begins visual search of *Titanic* site.
September 1, 1985	Ballard's group discovers wreckage of *Titanic*.
July 12–25, 1986	In a second expedition, Ballard photographs *Titanic* extensively.

1986	U.S. Congress passes RMS *Titanic* Maritime Memorial Act.
August 1987	A consortium later known as RMS Titanic, Inc., pays first visit to *Titanic* wreck and removes about 1,800 artifacts.
1988	Ballard begins Skerki Bank Deep Sea Project; finds a Roman shipwreck and an undersea volcano in the Mediterranean; conducts unsuccessful hunt for wreck of battleship *Bismarck*.
May 1989	Ballard establishes JASON Project to teach children about science; examines undersea volcano and Roman shipwreck *Isis* in first JASON Project broadcasts.
June 6, 1989	Ballard's group discovers wreckage of *Bismarck*.
1991	Ballard marries Barbara Earle; makes preliminary survey of Iron Bottom Sound off Guadalcanal and locates wrecks of 10 warships.
late July 1992	Ballard photographs wrecks in Iron Bottom Sound; makes preliminary visit to *Lusitania* wreck site.
1993	Ballard explores and photographs *Lusitania* wreck.
1994	A district court judge declares RMS Titanic, Inc., to be owner and salvor in possession of *Titanic* wreck.
1995	Ballard founds Institute for Exploration at Mystic (Connecticut) Aquarium.
1996	Ballard begins Black Sea Trade Project.

1997

Ballard retires from WHOI; reinvestigates Roman wrecks on Skerki Bank; videotapes three wrecks that might be Phoenician ships.

1998

RMS Titanic, Inc., brings large piece of *Titanic*'s hull to the surface; Walter Pitman and William Ryan of Columbia University theorize that a catastrophic flood struck the Black Sea 7,500 years ago.

May 1998

Ballard expedition looks for ships sunk during the Battle of Midway.

May 19, 1998

Ballard's group finds wreckage of aircraft carrier *Yorktown*.

1999

During his first underwater investigation of the Black Sea, Ballard finds signs of an ancient shoreline 550 feet (168 m) below the sea's present surface and other evidence that supports Pitman and Ryan's flood theory; reinvestigates Phoenician ships.

September 2000

During a second expedition to the Black Sea, Ballard finds possible remains of a Stone Age house and four well-preserved shipwrecks from the Roman and Byzantine periods.

November 2000

Ballard conducts an unsuccessful hunt for a Japanese midget submarine in the waters of Pearl Harbor, Hawaii.

May 2002

Ballard looks for the remains of John F. Kennedy's *PT-109* and finds a torpedo tube that belonged to the boat.

July 2002

Ballard becomes director of the Institute of Archaeological Oceanography at the University of Rhode Island.

2003   Ballard reinvestigates Black Sea wrecks with
                         new ROV, *Hercules*; revisits Skerki Bank
                         wrecks.

June 2004   Ballard rephotographs *Titanic* to demon-
                         strate damage done by salvagers.

2005   Ballard proposes making *Titanic* an under-
                         water museum that people can visit via the
                         Internet.

GLOSSARY

amphora (plural, amphorae) a large pottery jar used in ancient times for storing and shipping products such as wine and olive oil

artifact an object made by humans, such as a tool or utensil

basalt a dark, fine-grained rock, formed from cooling lava; it is believed to make up the bulk of the seafloor surface, as well as being deposited on land by volcanic eruptions

bathyscaphe a submersible consisting of a steel passenger sphere suspended from a large float that contains gasoline for buoyancy

black smoker a chimney on the seafloor, made of sulfide and other minerals, through which rises very hot water that appears dark because it contains large amounts of dissolved minerals

bow the front of a ship or boat

chemosynthesis the process of harnessing energy in certain chemicals, usually sulfur compounds or methane, to make food within a living thing's body. *Compare* PHOTOSYNTHESIS

continental drift a theory, first proposed by German meteorologist Alfred Wegener in 1915, stating that the continents can move horizontally on the Earth's surface and had different arrangements in early geologic times than they do now; it is the ancestor of the theory of plate tectonics

dynamic positioning system a system aboard some modern ships in which a computer sends signals to the ship's propellers that enable the ship to hold the same position even in rough seas

hemoglobin a red, iron-containing pigment that binds and transports oxygen; it is found in blood and in the body fluids of some sea creatures

hydrogen sulfide a compound of hydrogen and sulfur (H_2S) that usually exists as a poisonous gas with a rotten-egg smell; a small number of organisms can use it as an energy source

hydrothermal circulation a process by which seawater sinks through cracks in the Earth's crust, is heated by rocks in the mantle, and reemerges at hydrothermal vents, carrying dissolved minerals

hydrothermal vent a crack or fissure in the seafloor from which water heated by rock in the Earth's mantle pours up

Internet2 an advanced computer communication network established by a consortium of educational, industry, and government institutions

magma molten rock beneath the Earth's surface

mantle the layer of the Earth located below the crust, extending between about 20 miles (33 km) and 1,802 miles (2,900 km) below the surface

mesoscaphe a large submersible capable of carrying relatively large numbers of people to moderate depths and remaining submerged for weeks at a time

Mid-Ocean Ridge a continuous system of undersea ridges and rift valleys running through the world's oceans

mowing the lawn Robert Ballard's term for making a sonar survey of an underwater site by sailing a surface ship, towing the sonar device, back and forth over the site in overlapping tracks

photosynthesis the process by which green plants and some microorganisms capture light energy, usually from sunlight, and use it in chemical reactions that produce nourishment. *Compare* CHEMOSYNTHESIS.

plate tectonics a theory describing the creation, destruction, and movements of the Earth's crust that was proposed in 1967 and quickly accepted by the Earth science community; it is descended from Alfred Wegener's continental drift theory

port the left side of a ship or boat, as seen by a person standing on the craft and facing forward

radar (from *ra*dio *d*etection *a*nd *r*anging) a technology developed in the 1930s that uses electromagnetic waves to identify the range, speed, altitude, or direction of fixed or moving objects

rift valley a large, steep-sided valley made when crust subsides between two tectonic faults

ROV (Remotely Operated Vehicle) a robotic device controlled from a distance that is used to explore inhospitable environments such as the deep sea; for ocean exploration, it is usually controlled from a surface ship, to which it is attached with a fiber-optic tether

rudder the device that steers a ship or boat

rusticles Robert Ballard's term for dangling, stalactitelike deposits of rust (iron oxide) created by bacteria feeding on the iron in sunken shipwrecks

seafloor spreading   a theory proposed by Harry Hess in 1960, which states that new crust is created when molten rock pushes up through the seafloor at mid-ocean ridges and is destroyed when slabs of crust are pulled down into the mantle at undersea trenches; this process, driven by convection currents in the mantle, moves the crust of the Earth, including the continents, as if they were on a conveyor belt

seismology   the Earth science that studies earthquakes and other vibrations that move through the layers of the Earth, whether natural or produced by humans

sonar (from *so*und *n*avigation *a*nd *r*anging)   a tool that detects objects underwater by sending out sound waves and measuring the length of time the sounds take to return

starboard   the right side of a ship or boat, as seen by a person standing on the craft and facing forward

stern   the rear of a ship or boat

submersible   a vehicle designed to operate underwater, especially a small, untethered, human-carrying vehicle that is lowered from a mother ship and recalled to the ship each night; it is something like a small submarine

telepresence   Robert Ballard's term for the use of remotely controlled vehicles and devices to image and manipulate objects at a distance

teredo   a wormlike mollusk that eats wood; also called *shipworm*

thermistor   a device that detects changes in temperature

trench   an extremely deep valley in the ocean floor at the border of a tectonic plate

U-boat   (short for *Unterseeboot*) a German submarine

FURTHER RESOURCES

Books

Ballard, Robert D. *The Discovery of the* Titanic. New York: Warner Books, 1987.

> *An account of Robert Ballard's most famous discovery, the wreck of the famed ocean liner RMS Titanic. The liner sank after hitting an iceberg in the north Atlantic on April 14, 1912, killing 1,522 people. Ballard co-led the team that rediscovered the liner in 1985.*

——, with Rick Archbold. *The Discovery of the* Bismarck. New York: Warner Books, 1990.

> *Tells the story of Ballard's discovery of the wreckage of the German battleship in a 1989 expedition. Also describes the battle in May 1941 during which British warships sank the* Bismarck.

——, with Rick Archbold. *The Lost Ships of Guadalcanal.* New York: Warner Books, 1993.

> *Recounts Ballard's 1992 expedition to Iron Bottom Sound, last resting place of numerous ships sunk during naval battles near the island in late 1942. Includes information on the battles.*

——, and Rick Archbold. *The Lost Ships of Robert Ballard.* San Diego, Calif.: Thunder Bay Press, 2005.

> *Book well illustrated with photographs and paintings describes some of the ships Ballard has investigated, including* Titanic, Britannic, Lusitania, Bismarck, *and the ships of Guadalcanal.*

——, and Rick Archbold. *Return to Midway.* Washington, D.C.: National Geographic Society, 1999.

> *Describes Ballard's expedition to the Pacific island of Midway in May 1998, during which he discovered and photographed the remains of the aircraft carrier* Yorktown. *Includes information on the Battle of Midway (June 3–7, 1942).*

————, with Spencer Dunmore. *Exploring the* Lusitania. New York: Warner Books, 1995.

Describes Ballard's 1993 expedition to photograph the wreck of Lusitania, *sunk by a German torpedo in 1915. The book also presents the earlier history of* Lusitania *and its sister ship,* Mauretania.

————, with Toni Eugene. *Mystery of the Ancient Seafarers: Early Maritime Civilizations.* Washington, D.C.: National Geographic Society, 2004.

Provides background information on early seafaring cultures including the Phoenicians, Greeks, and Romans as well as describing Ballard's expeditions to study ancient shipwrecks in the Mediterranean and the Black Sea.

————, with Will Hively. *The Eternal Darkness: A Personal History of Deep-Sea Exploration.* Princeton, N.J.: Princeton University Press, 2000.

Ballard describes 20th-century advances in deep-sea exploration technology and some of the discoveries that resulted from these advances, including his personal role in many of them.

————, with Malcolm McConnell. *Explorations: A Life of Underwater Adventure.* New York: Hyperion, 1995.

Ballard's autobiography, in which he describes his career through the mid-1990s.

————, with Michael Hamilton Morgan. *Collision with History: The Search for John F. Kennedy's* PT-109. Washington, D.C.: National Geographic Society, 2002.

Describes Ballard's expedition to the Solomon Islands in May 2002, during which he searched for remnants of John F. Kennedy's patrol torpedo boat, PT-109, *and found a torpedo tube belonging to the boat. The book also recounts Kennedy's heroic actions after the boat was sunk by a Japanese destroyer in August 1943.*

————, with Michael Hamilton Morgan. *Graveyards of the Pacific.* Washington, D.C.: National Geographic Society, 2001.

Includes material on the World War II battles fought at Pearl Harbor, the Coral Sea, Midway, Guadalcanal, Truk Lagoon, the Philippine Sea, and Bikini Atoll as well as Ballard's expeditions to photograph sunken ships at several of these sites.

————, with Michael S. Sweeney. *Return to* Titanic. Washington, D.C.: National Geographic Society, 2004.

In this expedition, Ballard rephotographed Titanic *to demonstrate the damage done by salvagers during the 18 years since he had discovered the wreck.*

Glen, William. *The Road to Jaramillo: Critical Years of the Revolution in Earth Science.* Stanford, Calif.: Stanford University Press, 1982.

Firsthand account of the discoveries that established the theory of plate tectonics and convinced many Earth scientists of its correctness in the mid-1960s.

Kaharl, Victoria A. *Water Baby: The Story of* Alvin. New York: Oxford University Press, 1990.

Kaharl's account of Woods Hole Oceanographic Institution's famous submersible includes information on Robert Ballard's early career, which was closely involved with Alvin.

Kunzig, Robert. *Mapping the Deep: The Extraordinary Story of Ocean Science.* New York: W. W. Norton, 2000.

Describes some of the major advances in oceanography in the late 20th century, including the discovery of undersea evidence that established the theory of plate tectonics and the discovery of hydrothermal vents and the unusual animals that live around them.

Macdonald, John. *Great Battles of World War II.* New York: Smithmark Publishers, 1997.

Includes detailed descriptions, photographs, and maps of the sinking of the German battleship Bismarck *and the battles of Midway and Guadalcanal. Robert Ballard investigated shipwrecks resulting from all of these actions.*

O'Neill, William L. *World War II: A Student Companion.* New York: Oxford University Press, 1999.

For young people. Concise encyclopedia-type articles provide a quick reference on various aspects of the war.

"Robert Ballard." In *Encyclopedia of World Biography Supplement,* Vol. 19. Farmington, Mich.: Gale Group, 1999. Available online through Biography Resource Center. Accessed September 1, 2008.

Biographical profile of Ballard describes the highlights of his career.

Ryan, William, and Walter Pitman. *Noah's Flood: The New Scientific Discoveries about the Event that Changed History.* New York: Simon & Schuster, 1998.

Controversial book by two Columbia University geologists proposing that a gigantic flood occurred in the Black Sea about 7,500 years ago and gave rise to the story of Noah and other myths about tremendous floods. Robert Ballard found evidence that supported Ryan and Pitman's theory.

Yount, Lisa. *Alfred Wegener: Creator of the Continenal Drift Theory.* New York: Chelsea House, 2009.

> *For young people. The book outlines the life of the German meteorologist who created the continental drift theory, ancestor of the plate tectonics theory, and also explains how the latter theory, now widely accepted, developed out of Wegener's often-rejected ideas. Robert Ballard's early work as a marine geologist related to plate tectonics.*

————. *Modern Marine Science: Exploring the Deep.* New York: Chelsea House, 2006.

> *For young adults. Contains a chapter on Ballard. Some other chapters discuss matter related to Ballard's career, such as the development of plate tectonics theory and the history of the submersible* Alvin.

Internet Resources

Hind, Phil "Encyclopedia Titanica." Encyclopedia Titanica. Available onlne. URL: http://www.encyclopedia-titanica.org. Accessed September 1, 2008.

> *This site presents passenger and crew biographies, history, research, and discussions related to the famous ship and its disastrous sinking.*

"The JASON Project: Education through Exploration." The JASON Project. Available online. URL: http://www.jason.org/public/home. aspx. Accessed September 1, 2008.

> *Web site of Ballard's educational project for middle school students, founded in 1989; it is now a nonprofit subsidiary of the National Geographic Society. Materials on the site include a short biography of Ballard. Some curriculum materials are also available through the JASON Mission Center, part of the site.*

Mitchell, Jacqueline S. "Life Above Boiling." Scientific American Frontiers, Public Broadcasting System. Available online. URL: http://www.pbs.org/saf/1207/features/113.htm. Accessed September 1, 2008.

> *Set of interviews focuses on the hydrothermal vent ecosystems and the sulfide-digesting microorganisms that form their base.*

"Pushing the Boundaries of Knowledge." Mystic Aquarium & Institute for Exploration. Available online. URL: http://www.ife.org/DefaultPermissions/INSTITUTEFOREXPLORATION/tabid/274/Default.aspx. Accessed September 1, 2008.

Robert Ballard founded the Institute for Exploration as part of the Mystic (Connecticut) Aquarium in 1995. The IFE portion of the Mystic site includes information on the institute's research, its staff, Ballard (the institution's president), and the Immersion theater and educational program.

"RMS Titanic, Inc." RMS Titanic, Inc. Available online. URL: http://www.rmstitanic.net. Accessed September 1, 2008.

Web site of the organization that is legal owner and salvor in possession of the Titanic wreck. The site describes artifacts the group has taken, its museum exhibits, and its views on the ethics of salvaging and displaying objects from the wreck.

"*Titanic's* Lost Sister." NOVA, Station WGBH (Boston), Public Broadcasting System. 1997. Available online. URL: http://www.pbs.org./wgbh/nova/titanic/ballard.html. Accessed September 1, 2008.

Interview with Ballard describes some of his investigations of ancient shipwrecks and his plans to make RMS Titanic's sister ship, Britannic, into an underwater museum.

"Underwater and Maritime Archaeology." Cyberpursuits. Available online. URL: http://www.cyberpursuits.com/archeo/uw-arch.asp. Accessed September 1, 2008.

Site provides a wide variety of links to organizations and materials related to this subject.

Periodicals

Allen, Thomas B. "Return to the Battle of Midway." *National Geographic* 195 (April 1999): 80–103.

Allen's article focuses primarily on the June 1942 battle itself, but a long sidebar by Ballard describes his discovery of the aircraft carrier Yorktown, *which was sunk during the fighting.*

Ballard, Robert D. "The *Bismarck* Found." *National Geographic* 176 (November 1989): 622–637.

Pictures and text describe Ballard's discovery of the remains of the German battleship in June 1989.

———. "A Celebration of the Sea." *Popular Science* 246 (May 1995): 9–10.

Ballard offers many reasons why the sea is valuable to humankind.

———. "Dive into the Great Rift." *National Geographic* 147 (May 1975): 604–615.

Ballard describes his descent in the submersible Alvin *to examine a rift valley in the Mid-Atlantic Ridge, a site of seafloor spreading, during Project FAMOUS (French-American Mid-Ocean Undersea Study) in 1974.*

———. "Deep Black Sea." *National Geographic* 199 (May 2001): 52–68.

Recounts Ballard's discoveries in the Black Sea, including exceptionally well-preserved ancient shipwrecks and evidence for an ancient flood that may have inspired the Biblical story of Noah.

———. "High-Tech Search for Roman Shipwrecks." *National Geographic* 193 (April 1998): 32–41.

In this brief article, Ballard summarizes his early discoveries on Skerki Bank, an area of the Mediterranean containing wrecks of several Roman ships.

———. "How We Found *Titanic.*" *National Geographic* 168 (December 1985): 696–719.

Ballard tells how a French-U.S. expedition, of which he was coleader, discovered the world's most famous shipwreck in 1985.

———. "A Long Last Look at *Titanic.*" *National Geographic* 170 (December 1986): 698–727.

Ballard returned to the famous wreck in 1986 to photograph it more thoroughly than had been possible during his first visit, using a combination of the submersible Alvin *and remotely operated robotic vehicles that Ballard's team of scientists had designed.*

———. "The Search for *PT-109.*" *National Geographic* 202 (December 2002): 78–89.

Recounts Ballard's hunt for wreckage of John F. Kennedy's patrol torpedo boat and his recovery of a torpedo tube from the boat; includes a memorial sketch of his brother by Senator Edward Kennedy.

———. "Window on Earth's Interior." *National Geographic* 150 (August 1976): 228–249.

Describes Ballard's 1976 expedition to the Cayman Trough, in the Caribbean, where he dived in Alvin *to study the geology of the area.*

———, and J. Frederick Grassle. "Strange World without Sun." *National Geographic* 156 (November 1979): 680–704.

Ballard and others, including marine biologists, further explored the unique ecosystems that live around deep-sea hydrothermal vents with additional Alvin *dives in 1979.*

Conant, Eve. "In Search of Noah's Ark." *Newsweek International,* July 21, 2003.

> *Recounts Ballard's research in the Black Sea, including discovery of evidence supporting the theory that a catastrophic flood may have occurred in the area 7,500 years ago, giving rise to the story of Noah's Ark and other flood myths.*

Corliss, John B., and Robert D. Ballard. "Oases of Life in the Cold Abyss." *National Geographic* 152 (October 1977): 441–456.

> *Article pictures and describes the amazing life forms that Ballard, Corliss, and others discovered around hydrothermal vents in the deep sea near the Galápagos Rift in 1977.*

De Jonge, Peter. "Being Bob Ballard." *National Geographic* 205 (May 2004): 116–129.

> *A good recent profile of Ballard, stressing his research in the Black Sea and Mediterranean. The article describes how Ballard handles the obstacles that often delay his expeditions.*

Friedrich, Otto, and Natalie Angier. "After 73 Years, a Titanic Find." *Time* 126 (September 16, 1985): 68–70.

> *Describes Ballard's 1985 discovery of the sunken ocean liner* Titanic.

Golden, Frederic. "Man with Titanic Vision." *Discover,* January 1987, 51–62.

> *Dated but exceptionally detailed and well-written biographical profile of Ballard.*

Heirtzler, J. R. "Where the Earth Turns Inside Out." *National Geographic* 147 (May 1975): 586–603.

> *Heirtzler, the chief U.S. scientist involved in Project FAMOUS, provides background on the French-U.S. expedition to a rift valley in the Mid-Atlantic Ridge, an undersea mountain range. The project's aim was to look for direct proof of the theory of plate tectonics, which states that Earth's crust is created in such valleys.*

Lehrer, Eli. "Deep-Sea Explorer Brings History to Life." *Insight on the News* 15 (May 3, 1999): 21.

> *Fairly extensive interview with Ballard, including both his background and his current research.*

Macdonald, Ken C. "Exploring the Global Mid-Ocean Ridge: A Quarter-Century of Discovery." *Oceanus,* March 1998. Also available online. URL: http://www.whoi.edu/oceanus/viewarticle.do?id=2512.

Includes descriptions of Project FAMOUS and the 1977 discovery of hydrothermal vents and vent animals. Discusses the importance of mapping and studying mid-ocean ridges to learn about plate tectonics; also describes ongoing ridge research.

Matthews, Samuel W. "New World of the Ocean." *National Geographic* 160 (December 1981): 792–832.

This article on new technology for deep-sea exploration includes one of Ballard's first descriptions of his proposed Argo-Jason *system.*

Mone, Gregory. "What's Eating the *Titanic*?" *Popular Science* 265 (July 1, 2004): 42.

Short article lists the causes of the Titanic *wreck's deterioration in the years since Robert Ballard discovered it.*

Murphy, Jamie. "Down into the Deep." *Time* 128 (August 11, 1986): 48–54.

Murphy explains how several scientists, including Robert Ballard, are using new technology to explore shipwrecks and look for treasure in the deep sea.

Murphy, Joy Waldron. "The Search for the *Titanic* Is Over, But Now a Rush for the 'Gold' Has Begun." *Smithsonian* 17 (August 1986): 56–65.

Portrays competition for salvage rights to the wreck of Titanic *that followed Robert Ballard's discovery of the liner.*

Schrope, Mark. "Welcome to Museum *Titanic* (Please Don't Touch)." *Popular Science* 267 (July 1, 2005): 49.

Describes Robert Ballard's plans for making Titanic *a virtual underwater museum.*

INDEX